Praise for *Life Lessons from the Heart of Horses*

"Through enchanting storytelling, Kathy Pike immerses us in the magical relationship that humans can experience with horses. They reveal themselves as shamans and teachers who help us to build positive relations, become intelligent and compassionate leaders, and even bring healing, understanding, and clarity. This book is a rare and beautiful journey into Kathy's artistry of coaching with horses; her storytelling transforms the reader into experiencing the opening of their hearts through the horses' way."

—Aldo Civico, PhD, anthropologist and executive coach

"Praise to Kathy Pike! What a delightful book rich with stories of life lessons she has gleaned from her special horse herd, not only of her personal treasured adventures, but also of her profound work coaching with horses that changes people's lives. I feel like I get a glimpse into her passionate life with horses and I am on the journey with her. Each chapter ends with self-reflective questions that you can journal about, making the book all the more powerful. From leadership to self-compassion, dancing with horses to living life fully, she offers so many inspirations. I highly recommend this important book that chronicles the horse as healer and teacher."

—Ariana Strozzi Mazzucchi, founder of Equine Guided Education

"What a beautiful book! From wild child to the direct, smart, and honest voice of the spirit of creation that she has become, Kathy Pike shares a lifetime of love for the giving and benevolent nature of horses as guides, healers, and teachers. They show us the way to the sustainable health, well-being, and vitality that are essential to solving the many problems facing our world. This book is a celebration of the path of mutual benefit that is now necessary for the sake of life itself, and an essential reading experience."

—Francis Rico, author of *A Shaman's Guide to Deep Beauty* and founder of Applying Shamanism

Life Lessons

from the

Heart *of* Horses

Life Lessons
from the
Heart *of* Horses

How Horses Teach Us About Relationships and Healing

Kathy Pike

author of *Hope . . . From the Heart of Horses*

Skyhorse Publishing

Skyhorse Publishing books may be purchased in bulk at special discounts for sales promotion, corporate gifts, fund-raising, or educational purposes. Special editions can also be created to specifications. For details, contact the Special Sales Department, Skyhorse Publishing, 307 West 36th Street, 11th Floor, New York, NY 10018 or info@skyhorsepublishing.com.

Skyhorse® and Skyhorse Publishing® are registered trademarks of Skyhorse Publishing, Inc.®, a Delaware corporation.

Visit our website at www.skyhorsepublishing.com.

10 9 8 7 6 5 4 3 2

Library of Congress Cataloging-in-Publication Data is available on file.

Cover design by Daniel Brount and Kathy Pike
Cover photograph by Tony Stromberg

Print ISBN: 978-1-5107-6283-1
Ebook ISBN: 978-1-5107-6284-8

Printed in China

I dedicate this book to all of the horses, those in captivity and those who roam free—may you experience love, honor, and respect from humankind.

Contents

Introduction

THE POWER OF NATURE

I grew up in the state of Maine. During the summer months, I tended to the family garden. I swam in the ocean and hiked in the woods to harvest fiddleheads. Late summer mornings were spent in the thick of wild blueberry bushes with instructions to fill my container with the deep purple-blue nuggets of sweetness that later would become pies or sprinkled over cereal. At night, I slept outside under the stars. The night skies would often close up with clouds, and the sprinkles of rain would send me onto the front porch.

Autumn was the time for picking, polishing, and bagging apples that I then sold at the roadside. The bruised or dropped apples became every imaginable sugar-sweetened dish, made with the best baking apple of all time, the MacIntosh. In the winter, I continued to seek time outside. After school, I would grab my ice skates and hike back to a pond in the woods. I would relish the solitude of the late winter day; the sun was dim and soft, the ice was hard and cold, and all I could hear were the sounds of my sharp blades slicing into the glass-like surface. My highly sensitive spirit needed the getaway. I found solace in nature, far away from human incongruences and the sounds of traffic. My first experiences with horses included feeding apples to the neighbor's horse, riding bareback through apple orchards with my best friend on her old farm horse, and getting to go on an occasional group ride through 4-H, America's largest young development organization.

As I grew older, my need for nature did not diminish; it was not an option for me but a needed experience. In my twenties, I spent a considerable amount of time climbing the mountains in Grand Teton National Park in Wyoming, exploring Northern California's deep woods, and hiking and backpacking through Utah's and Arizona's deserts. Additionally, I loved running rivers in the wild and vast regions of southeast Alaska, and skiing anywhere I could find fresh powder.

Going into the wild from four days to three weeks at a time, completely disconnected from society, current events, and news removes all the conveniences of society. Entirely dependent on myself, or those I was with, my daily life-cycle aligned with nature: I rose at dawn, rested in the heat of the day, and slept shortly after nightfall. I became so connected to the rhythm and way of natural life and the freedom to allow my spirit to be expansive in the vast and inspiring landscapes that I found significant discomfort within any building's four walls upon returning home. Feeling overwhelmed in small, tight gatherings with friends only highlighted how open my entire being had become from living outside for weeks.

The extended time I spent in Mother Nature built a strong foundation for my future connection and understanding of horses. When I lived at Jenny Lake Lodge in Teton National Park, I would hike to the lakes and sit in the trees in the early spring months. I would focus on the numerous bird songs, their voices bringing aliveness to the woods that had only recently lost the remaining winter snow layers into the deep, rich, and moist earth. During times like that, I would feel an indescribable peacefulness within my psyche and mental state of being; in those moments, time felt like it stood still, and my consciousness felt as if it merged with the plants and animals, sounds, and earth herself.

Simultaneously, as I felt less separate and more connected with all around me, I also felt more present in my body, often feeling a strong, steady pulse of life force energy moving through me. The edges of the plants, trees, mountains, streams, and flowers would soften and become much less defined to my naked eye. A sense of floating within the environment versus traveling through it would shift and alter my mind-space and bring me into a timeless expression of my existence. These moments were utterly delicious to my mind, body, and spirit. I had become more like a horse in my energy than like a human.

Other times in my life when I did not live in wilderness areas, I would reinvent these experiences only by going to the nearby woods where I would sit, breathe, smell, listen to the diverse sounds of nature, and wait. Before long, I would again see the edges of the trees meld and diffuse, losing definition, as if I was in a self-induced dream-state of reality. At the time, I never entirely understood it, although I always felt renewed and refreshed afterward.

After exploring many wilderness adventures in my twenties, I found myself hypothermic on a river trip on the Tatshenshini River in Alaska. The morning after, exhausted but out of danger, I watched and listened to the sound of calving icebergs. During this defining moment, I gave thanks for pulling out of the hypothermia and promised myself that when I got back home, I would focus my life on giving back to others. It was time. Two months later, I was back in Utah, and I had signed up for massage school. My spiritual and personal development path officially began. At twenty-eight, I was on a path of healing and a journey to my authenticity.

Little did I know then that my path in helping others would eventually circle back around to nature, connecting people to the most profound and compelling aspects of themselves through engaging with horses in nontraditional ways. What I knew and understood naturally from my years of being in nature and as a highly empathic, intuitive, and sensitive individual would eventually become part of my teaching for others as I partnered with horses as my co-teachers.

Since that defining moment watching icebergs flip in the ocean half of my life's journey ago, I have spent most of my time on a healing path. I have deepened my awareness of the physical body and how to heal old trauma. I became a life coach and have provided and received a tremendous amount of growth in the process. Meditation and yoga have played a part in my life, helping me experience a more profound connection with myself and connect even more profoundly beyond the physical world. I have gathered the courage and vulnerability to find my true self, my authentic nature, uncluttered by the expectations or conditioning of others through my interaction with my herd of horses.

HORSES ARE MY TEACHERS

Horses have been my most exceptional teachers in healing, empowerment, and finding my authentic self. Following their lead and embracing their way of being in the world has brought me back to a place that I treasure: I know who I am. My deepest gratitude goes out to Mother Earth and all of the intense and subtle moments of connection and beauty, empowerment, and peace that I have found on her shores and mountaintops. Without the guidance and conversations that I have had with horses, I would still be a bit of a lost soul, searching for my true self, just like many other individuals on earth currently are.

Many years ago, horses came into my life when I was writing my first book, *Pathways to a Radiant Self*, along Oregon's coast. The day after 9/11, with New York City buried in ash and reeling from the trauma of the Twin Towers coming down, I sat on the beach experiencing one of the most pristine days of the year. The sun was soft; the ocean barely created waves that gently caressed the shoreline. I watched a woman with her hair flowing in the wind ride down the wide sandy beach, bareback, on a beautiful chestnut-colored horse. Behind her followed a younger horse with just a rope connecting them. The scene was a brilliant spectacle of freedom. As she returned from her graceful canter down the beach, I introduced myself to her. She invited me to her farm, where I met a horse named Hope.

I began working with Hope, and within just a week or so, I took lessons from a Natural Horseman. As we worked in a round pen, I was instructed to send Hope around the pen's edge as I stood in the center. Then I was told to ask her to walk, trot, and then canter. When I asked Hope, a shimmery red and fit horse, to canter, she instead turned abruptly toward me. With her head held high and her mane tossing in the momentum of her sudden turn, she stopped. Her power and beauty overtook me, and I felt my entire presence leaving my body. Hope had simply done what I asked her to do. I did not realize it at the time, but my body position had given her a cue to turn in. Because I was new to understanding the body language of a horse, I did not understand. The forward-moving, formidable energy of a 1,000-pound being coming straight at me was more than my body or brain would take. Fear flooded my thinking mind, and I felt myself unconsciously leave my body, the center of my being, to escape the perceived danger that was approaching me. My physical body was still in the round pen, but my consciousness had left.

Hope showed me my unconscious response when confronted with power, authority, or big energy. My response was to lower into an old pattern of dissociative behavior. My presence would simply leave my body as a coping strategy. I lost my power in these situations and let others take advantage of, control, or influence me into actions that I intuitively knew were not right. I received a life-changing gift from the red mare, which helped me to see a pattern and move through and beyond it on a visceral level. This encounter retrained my brain and my body into a new behavioral response to power, authority, or big energy. New neuropathways of communication between my mind and body became activated, and I learned how to stay fully present with Hope's significant energy. This first lesson with Hope was a life-changing event for me, and bells and whistles went off as I saw personal and leadership development potential while working with the mare. In twenty minutes, she taught me what I had been working on shifting and changing for several years.

As a life coach of many years, I searched for a way to bring people into nature and empower them through a combination of coaching and firsthand experience. I had found it, and I was thrilled. I continued to work with the powerful mare under a trainer's instruction and eventually understood how a horse thinks, moves, and relates to another being. Twenty years later, there is a growing trend toward utilizing the wisdom of nature and her creatures to teach people how to de-stress, ignite their creativity, become empowered, and learn how to lead in a completely different way than the social norm demonstrates.

I bring people together with horses to learn, in the moment, with a 1,000-plus-pound live, sentient being as their source of instant feedback. It is provoking and often life-changing work. This book will share many stories of just how this happens and the philosophies that support it. Through reading, reflecting, and using the concepts I share with you, it is my hope that you will learn new ways to lead your life and also become a leader for others. I hope you stop searching outside of yourself for answers and come back into your body and being, using intuition to resource your power with elegance and ease, just like a horse.

My relationship with horses has evolved exponentially since those late summer days back in Maine, riding bareback with my friend and feeding the dropped apples to the neighbor's horse. Additionally, many years have passed since I wrote my first book, *Hope . . . From the Heart of Horses: How Horses Teach Us About Presence and Awareness*, which offers stories demonstrating the horse's capacity to heal and expand the human heart. Writing this book has been more touching than anticipated. The words and stories in this book reveal a deep partnership that I have found with horses. It humbles me that I have had the gift of living these stories and writing this book to share with you. I have lived a unique way with horses for the last fifteen years of my life. The horses have trusted me to be a spokesperson for the wisdom and intelligence they have to offer us.

This book takes you on a more in-depth journey through a collection of short stories based on the human-horse connection and interaction. I hope that your heart is touched, your curiosity ignited, and you are called to new actions and approaches with all animals in reading these stories. Additionally, I trust that you will recognize moments expressed in this text similar to your path with nature, her animals, and especially horses. All of these stories are based on real events. Only the name of the horse, person, or location is modified or slightly altered for privacy reasons.

Mahatma Gandhi once said, "The greatness of a nation and its moral progress can be judged by the way its animals are treated." This book represents a new way to be with horses. An approach that is deeply engaged with the communication and instant biofeedback that horses offer their handlers. In evolving our way of being with animals, we also raise the collective consciousness of the world. We become a community that treats each other and animals with kindness, respect, understanding, and honor.

This book is presented in four sections. In Part I, you will explore the ever-changing relationships within a herd. New members create disruptions and a reorganization of attention and connections. Changes in the environment affect how the herd functions as a whole, and a wild mustang, hard-wired and living wild until he was five, attempts to manage the strong-headed and often pushy mares that enter the domesticated herd. These stories help the reader find metaphors of how they may function in groups or families, and they may relate to the different horses as representative of the humans in their life.

Part II offers a deeper understanding of the true nature of horses. A horse's big heart, patience, and propensity to be fully present provides a space for the release of tension and stress in a human so that well-being can emerge. Horses are natural healers to each other and the human spirit. The heartfelt connection can be ever-expanding, the release of old deep-seated emotions cathartic, while the loss of a herd member deeply profound. Those individuals more scientifically oriented may say that animals do not have emotion. The feelings felt by horses are not processed in the same way as human emotions. They move through different states of being with more grace and ease than the typical person because they do not mentalize feelings. They feel something, they express what is needed, and they move on. Horses' bonds also go deep, and their connection is stable—each member of a herd integrating and processing the collective's dynamic in their way. This part explores the silent and subtle ways that horses move us to receive their energy and presence and return to our hearts.

Part III will also stir your heart and give you a new view of horses as influential teachers and healers for humans. Horses often give instant biofeedback to humans. When a person is willing to listen to what a horse may offer, there is an opportunity to learn about the hidden aspects of the self that need to surface and be acknowledged so that transformation and change can occur. I invite you to join the journey and story of many individuals. Experience their transformations as they allowed the horse to be their teacher during my Coaching with Horses programs.

Part IV leads you to explore what it truly means for a horse to be a wild spirit and what is required when taken from your family and natural habitat and put into the chaotic human world. Join a little black Spanish mustang on his journey of domestication. You will surely understand the truly giving and benevolent nature of all horses through a once wild stallion.

I trust you will find your way to the stories that resonate with you. You need not read this book in any particular order. You may skip around between parts and read each story on its own. I invite you to become more curious about the new ways to explore and partner with all animals, and ultimately with each other, to create more reliable connections and understanding. We are taught how the world works at a very young age. The truth of the matter is that you can make any world you want. You can be with the animals in any way that you wish. You choose how your heart leads and guides you in considering the heart of the horse, or any animal, in that process.

Horses are pure beings that seek harmony. They seldom mean any harm to any other horse or individual unless they are provoked, are in severe emotional or physical pain, or feel threatened. Horses conserve energy and focus on having cohesive understanding among their herd members because they understand that this is the way to move beyond surviving into a thriving status, growing their herd into sustainable health, well-being, and vitality.

Horses also offer healing and respite for those in need, including creatures they interact with and other herd members. A horse with a highly in-tune nature becomes alarmed when another is in distress, and as a collective, they find unique ways to heal and move through troubling times, often by their presence alone.

As a totem animal of power, horses teach us the importance of belonging and how leadership can be flexible and diverse. Although this book focuses on the topics of healing and relationships, you will find that to achieve these states, you must shift your energy from a dominant state of power into a heart-based understanding of the importance of community and herd.

My life has grown exponentially through living with and learning daily from my horses. Every horse that I have interacted with has taught me something about myself, how to be with others, or their unique way of living on earth. At home, I have offered coaching with horses work for many years. They are masters at being teachers for humans. I continue to be their student. I receive no respite from their teachings. They continually humble me through our interactions. Regardless if I am searching for stillness in my being when standing with them, drawing healthy and clear boundaries with powerful, demanding mares, or learning what my benevolent wild horse and once stallion needs for recognition, the horses teach me. They are characters in this beautiful unfolding play called life.

I put forth these stories with vulnerability and courage. The horses have taught me how to stand my ground and allow others to be who they need to be emotionally, mentally, and physically. If this book changes one person's approach to horses in this vast and quickly expanding world, I will know that I have been a voice for the voiceless and that I have fulfilled part of my purpose as an advocate for equine intelligence and as a member of the collective equine herd. May this book invite you into a new way of being with horses and may horses always be with you.

PART I
Relationship Dynamics

Jumping Crawdads

My friend walked down to the edge of the river before the big flood and noticed the crawdads were jumping out of the river—literally jumping out of the river and up onto the bank. When she told an official about this obscure behavior, he asked her what time it had happened. It turns out it was precisely the time the big wall of water released out of the mountains and was on its way down the canyon and to the plains, where it eventually hit the town of Longmont, Colorado.

Two days later, while people were frantically attempting to save their homes and find higher ground, my friend observed the Koi fish in her pond acting hyper and spastic, behaviors she had never seen before. I mentioned author Masaru Emoto's theory that water reflects the vibrational qualities of the thoughts and emotional patterns in the local environment. It made sense that the fish might behave this way when there was so much anxiety, adrenaline, and fear within the community.

The night the water came gushing down the riverbanks, taking houses, trailers, fences, and pretty much anything in its way downstream, I walked out to feed my horses before the catastrophic event. Each horse in the herd stood very quietly in their dry shelters. They watched my every move, not moving a muscle in their bodies, not even following me for the sweet feed like they usually do. Their eyes penetrated my being, bringing me to their wisdom and knowing.

I stopped for a moment and entered into the herd space and time, and then I felt "it," the solemn energy, stillness to the bone, and deep knowing of what was to come. The herd was listening to something that was happening in another world and miles away. My feet got heavy, and I stood with them in the silence, allowing my sensing to come alive. Then, I, too, began to hear and sense it. Something big was approaching. The herd did not look troubled, but instead intent on communicating this message. At that moment, I knew we were going to be safe and that the next twenty-four hours would be much bigger than anticipated. Shortly after, I canceled my plans to meet a friend. Thankfully I did, or I would have become stranded away from my home, possibly for days.

During the Colorado flood, animals had moved to higher ground. No elk or deer were floating down the washes. Like the crawdads, they had jumped to where it was safe. Humans often view these animal behaviors as separate from our experience. We say things such as, "Those animals are so intelligent. They have this extrasensory awareness. The animals know." Yes, indeed, this is right. Their brains are wired to listen to the nuances of changing temperatures, the moisture content in the air, and the vibrational patterns of the land itself. They have that capacity. And so do we. The only difference is that we have stopped listening, trusting, and allowing ourselves the time to drop into the wisdom we have.

In my twenties, I spent many weeks and months living in the woods. The high mountain peaks of Jackson Hole, Wyoming, became part of my being. I slept on the ground, walked on the earth, bathed in cold rivers, listened to the birds, and felt the climate on my skin. I had no cell phone, no television, no news channel to tap into so I would know how to dress. I seemed to do just fine.

Wyoming's red rock slot canyons kept me listening on all levels; the waters of the Grand Canyon were soothing to my spirit. I could sense when my rain gear needed to be at hand, when an animal was watching me, and when I needed to stop and listen more deeply, find shelter, or bask in the sun that would disappear soon. When the life of the woods and all of the critters became still and quiet, I paid attention, as it always seemed that shortly after that, big rains, storms, winds, or significant changes in the weather would occur. Often, I would become one with the wildlife around me, finding myself only yards away from moose, elk, deer, and bears. Even now, I seldom spend time in nature without seeing or experiencing wildlife. This deep connection to Mother Earth and all of her creatures is still in me.

However, I have been urbanized. I made a conscious choice as my business grew to move from a more remote natural environment to the front range of the Rocky Mountains. My ranch is in the country, so I still feel the vibrations of the earth and the animals, but I also feel the vibration of society. Cars, planes, electrical lines, distant trains, cell phones, and a fast-paced lifestyle all exist here. When night arrives, I sink back into Mother Earth, listen to the birds, and feel the depth of the tree roots on my property.

One of the philosophies for being with horses is that they bring us back to the earth, to the land, to feel the energy and vibration of our natural environment. The horses help us to be open to the wisdom of our instinctual knowledge. If we allow our sensory awareness to be alive and integrated into our consciousness, the result is a wisdom that is much greater and more complete than just intellect. This level of wisdom is integrated fully with all that is around us. It sees all as part of us. This integrated wisdom moves beyond the "I" and into the "we" and is in full communication with the needs of the earth, the climate, and all living creatures. It tells us when to jump out of the river.

The energy of a herd tells us what is going on in the environment at a more heightened level. When several horses are displaying the same mood and body language, a human will do well to tap into the energy they are expressing and heed the messages. Their intelligence can lead us to better decisions. Without the willingness to open our sensory awareness, we can only be observers in this journey called life.

Animals are not separate. They sometimes become less sensitive or in tune when we remove them from their natural environments and rhythms of the earth. Corazon, my wild horse, is a perfect example of this. Over the years, his inner wildness and highly sensitive nature have slowly become less accentuated through living in the human world. However, it is still there. He engages it when he needs it. He is solid in himself; his inner freedom and wisdom shall never be taken away from him. My six acres, surrounded by roads and barn lights at night, certainly cannot provide the same stimulation as the big starry sky of the Pryor Mountains of Montana. He, too, has been urbanized.

At this moment, while writing these words, my inner wildness longs to return to the woods to have that innate deeper connection with all that is alive in those environments. However, if I follow Cor's lead, I know that no matter where my feet are standing on the earth, I determine what I listen to and how connected or disconnected from my wisdom and all of the life around me I want to be. I prefer to listen to and be part of my herd. I choose to listen to the earth and nature over that of the vibrations of urbanization.

REFLECTIONS

In the stillness and the bigness of nature, if you listen carefully and sense what is happening, you can merge to discern a deeper understanding of your environment. Being a part of a herd heightens the collective awareness and knowledge of the energy affecting both the individual and the group. Finding and working with human "herds" can also reflect changes to be aware of; it's a matter of tuning in to the subtleties and nuances that reveal themselves at a different level of perception and then choosing to make changes when necessary.

- When and how does your herd or Mother Nature communicate with you?
- Where do you connect and listen deeply to the essence of earth and all of its creatures?
- What is your commitment to living with your senses wide open?
- What do you choose to listen to?
- The next time your body says jump (just like a crawdad), or be still and wait, are you willing to listen?

Integrating the Herd Amid Escalating Emotions— Communication and Leadership

Herd dynamics provide excellent examples of interactions that can bring great insights and realizations. In my herd, I have attracted powerful lead mares who are seeking a herd in which they can become the central governing member and also instinctive and aware geldings who are very responsive. Watching the dynamics between the mares and geldings in a herd has helped me understand the concept of affect contagion (when you unconsciously entrain with the emotions and feelings that others have activated in their system and are expressing) and emerging energy, as well as lack of awareness and clear communication, all of which can escalate into unproductive states. A horse who came to my ranch became my teacher in both dynamics.

Scotch, a bright red, solid, and energized hot quarter horse was with us for a workshop one month previously and proved to be an excellent guide and teacher for my students. My horse, Diva, and I had ridden Colorado mountain trails many times with Scotch and her person. Having known each other from previous farms, the two horses got on brilliantly, so when the facility Scotch was living at closed, she came to stay at my ranch.

I had hoped to have Scotch integrated into my entire herd soon after her arrival. I allowed everyone to meet over the fence for several days.

Their noses could touch and begin the process of saying hello. Because Diva and Scotch were already friends, my next step was to introduce Scotch to Ginger, a five-year-old who had a lot of fire and life in her. The two red mares bonded immediately, like two friends who had been separated for years.

However, because of their strong personalities, they continued to have a conversation about who was going to be lead mare. The ranch soon went from a peaceful sanctuary to one filled with two mares crying and screeching; if not at each other, they would screech at me if I were ten minutes late to feeding time. Once a week, I would go out in the morning to find fence posts bent, gates broken, and fences torn down.

Keeping the two of them together was no longer working. Between vying for the lead and both having a tremendous amount of energy to begin with, the affect contagion ran rampant, and their ability to settle down and mellow out was not coming to fruition. The two horses continued to feed off each other to the point where the rest of the herd wanted nothing to do with them. After three repairs to fencing and additional attempts to help them find their way through their relationship, I finally decided that it was not going to happen. Scotch had gotten over Ginger and was now consistently pushing her away; this only pushed Ginger's attachment buttons, causing more anxiety in her body.

I came to several realizations from the behaviors that these two horses exhibited in their relationship with each other.

1. Take control of how your body responds

When you do not have the governing power to control your bodily emotions and feelings, it can lead to the experience of affect contagion, eventually escalating to unproductive energy and wasting emotions that keep you in a tailspin. Affect contagion is very common in herds of horses. The two red mares fed off each other, escalating their energy and emotions into unproductive states. This is very common; when fear arises in one horse, it can send the rest of the horses in the herd into a state of panic.

Highly sensitive individuals can also experience these phenomena, usually when they have not learned how to set their personal space and energy daily and track how they feel. The highly sensitive human often behaves like a horse, and unconsciously takes on the mood and feelings of others. One must learn to master the skill of sorting out their feelings and where they are truly coming from.

2.   Understand co-leadership

Can two lead mares successfully live together when they are mature enough to understand the flow of co-leadership? This would require each horse to understand their leadership skills and have the ego strength to step back when a situation requires another's skills. In other words, mutual respect.

Living in harmony requires a maturity of knowing one's place. If one strong-headed individual within a collective cannot have reverence and respect for a wiser elder, this cannot be achieved. If a strong-headed individual is not willing or able to recognize when to follow and when to lead, it also cannot be achieved. The two red mares, both with strong wills and fiery temperaments, never reached this place of understanding.

I see this dynamic occur often in the human world, particularly with humans who have horses. There can be competitive energy that will arise when one feels it is time to get above another. If you find yourself in this mindset, ask and answer the questions at the end of this chapter.

3. Things change, so stay flexible

A student said to me the other day, "When I take a horse in, it is forever." This statement took me aback because I recalled that years ago I said the very same thing. Now that I've had the experience of placing three "head-strong" mares in new homes, along with trying to integrate a new one into the herd, I realize the naivety of this statement.

First, it locks you into a promise that you may not be able to keep. Second, it assumes that all relationships are meant to be long-term. And third, it leaves no open door for one to hear the wishes of herd members and their cries for a new situation when their spirit and soul are not flourishing. Although this statement expresses the human's sense of loyalty, true loyalty is recognizing what is best for all parties when making needed changes for the welfare of all, even when painful to the human heart.

A few days later, I tried to integrate Scotch with the boys. That did not go well. My mustang Corazon (who was a wild and free stallion until he was five and a half years old—the age is important because the older they are, the harder to train) has become more and more protective of "his herd." Once in the field together, he decided he needed to run Scotch off immediately and continue to run her down, demonstrating aggressive and dominant behavior. The entire herd was a galloping frenzy. You can imagine my disappointment and then growing concern for the welfare of Scotch as well as Moon, my elder horse who was caught up in the chase. Eventually, Scotch came running back into the paddocks with Corazon right at her tail. She did a quick turnaround and flew out of the paddock, and I was able to shut the gate, leaving Corazon locked in, snorting, pawing, and prancing around. Scotch is a smart mare.

Everyone was hot and worked up for such a cold day. I had to work hard not to beat myself up for not having better timing and communication with Corazon before all three were put in the same pasture together. I do believe Corazon got the message when he spent the rest of the day in the paddock with Moon beside him for company. His displeasure was expressed as he put his butt to everyone and stared out at the opposite pasture. The three mares all ate from the hay I had in the field, all three of them going from one pile to the next together. Moon stood utterly exhausted, head hanging low and body heavy. The elder of the herd laid down and released leadership to those with more energy.

My lesson was obvious. I had talked *at* Moon and Corazon about what was going to happen, how they needed to behave, and accept her: "Scotch needs a home. She is not becoming mine, but we need to welcome her onto this ranch. I don't want any problems with this, and we must welcome her with kindness." What I failed to do is truly hear their opinion on the matter. If I had been attentive, I would have noticed and also heeded the warning from Moon as he proceeded to go over to the fence line, pin his ears at Scotch, and turn around and give me a dirty look. He gets so jealous. I would have also paused to fully understand Corazon's eyes intently staring at Scotch and watching her every move around Ginger. Instead, I went unconscious, just wanting everyone to get along. Having Corazon in my life and working with him in herds has been a demanding experience. He is not like domesticated horses and never will be. Thinking I could integrate the herd on *my timeline* was wrong. My herd consists of three strong horses, all having their agendas and needs. When these needs are filled, harmony prevails; when they are not, chaos reigns.

How do we work in these situations where such strong beings fully express their needs and demand they are met? Communication has to be a two-way street. When we get stressed and just want things to be "fine," it is a sign that we need to slow down and not push to make it fine. Animals are not objects. If we want to live with them and see them as sentient beings, we can't just maneuver them around and expect them to comply with our will.

We all slip from being conscious to becoming unconscious and into old patterns of behavior. Unfortunately, there is always a cost when we do that. Usually, the damage can be healed, mended, or restored. I trust it will with each of the members of my herd. The main thing is to see and catch the behaviors we engage in that affect others and then make significant changes.

I now set my intention to go to the herd each day and to stop talking *at* them and telling them how things are going to be. Instead, I open my being to what they have to say to me. I get into horse time. I read their body language and sense what is going on within the herd. I watch more closely and listen. Now, I enter into their living space with the request of "What do you want to share with me today? What are your desires for the herd today?"

REFLECTIONS

I hope this story inspires you to look at your herd and their dynamics or to look at your life and the uncomfortable dynamics you are playing out, consciously or unconsciously, so that you can become more aware and proactive. If we always work from the position of dominance, we are often unconscious of the needs of others, which can lead to two strong heads butting up against each other. When you start to focus on your personal space and energy and take proactive steps in developing the skills to move beyond unconscious response, affect contagion, co-dependency, competition, lack of awareness, and rigidness, you will find much more grace. When you find yourself negatively responding to situations of co-leadership, ask yourself the following questions:

- What am I competing for?
- What keeps me from respecting the elder or the more experienced person?
- What can I learn here without having to get into resistant mind patterns that create separation from others?
- What uncomfortable energy in my body am I not addressing that would reveal my unconscious motivations?

It's All About Timing

Many years ago, when I got my very first horse, Moon, who was ten years old at the time, I boarded him at a public facility. To my astonishment and dismay, when he arrived at the new ranch where I was to keep him, he looked thirty years old. He was infested with ticks, underweight, and utterly depressed. Seeing him look so broken, a vast difference from the vibrant, healthy, muscular-chested horse with bright eyes that I had first met and agreed to take, was heartbreaking. It turned out that his previous owners had sent him to a holding facility through the winter months before he came to me. Before that, he had lived on a 100,000-acre cattle ranch. The abrupt move to an unknown holding facility took a toll on his heart, health, and overall well-being.

The reason he had to leave the large ranch was that he could no longer canter. On a large working cattle ranch with thousands of acres, if a horse can't earn his keep, he has to go. I had asked if we could wait until spring to bring him to me in Colorado. I was naïve to realize what it meant when the woman who gifted him to me said they would put him into a holding facility for the winter.

Once he arrived in Colorado, I asked the barn manager how we would integrate my depressed and underweight horse into the herd. He said, "Simple, we just throw him in there with all of the other geldings. Everyone (about twenty horses) will sort it out." Intuitively, I felt uneasy about his reply. My gut said it would not turn out well. However, because I lacked enough horse experience at the time, I released my power to the barn manager and let him do as he wanted.

Over the next several days, Moon was beaten up by the herd, receiving many nicks, bites, and bruises. One day, when I pulled him out of the herd, I swore to myself that if I ever had the privilege to own a ranch, I would find safer and less traumatic ways to integrate horses into one herd. Over several weeks, I fed Moon separate from the herd. I put raw garlic in his bowl along with carrot and grain. He would choose the grain, and much to my surprise, the garlic. I picked off as many ticks as I could, and the rest fell off from the garlic. Moon began to recover. He put on weight, his muscle tone developed as he walked in the pastures, and he regained his confidence.

Today, I am blessed to have a sweet little horse property where I manage my horses. I still believe that there is no need for any horse to suffer while being integrated into a new herd. It does not mean it is always easy. In fact, it can be very challenging. My knowledge has grown exponentially on this matter as I have integrated four females and several males into the herd at different times over the last seven years.

***

After the big floods in Colorado that wiped out many towns and destroyed canyon roads, I adopted a pregnant mare from a man who had lost his home and pastures. Layla came to the herd defensive and protective of her unborn foal. I kept her away from the other herd members, and she would only go to pasture by herself.

I have several pens with gates on every side of each pen. Some of the pens are interconnected. One day while mucking, I accidentally left one gate open. Layla dashed out of her pen through the next pen and went out to the broad field in the back. The other horses had just been let out and were grazing. Then Corazon, my mustang, and Moon, the elder horse, took it upon themselves to run Layla down. I had never seen this level of cruel behavior from either of them before.

Getting involved was too dangerous. The screeching, kicking, biting, and speed of their thousand-pound bodies were not a mix I wanted to get tangled up in. I opened the gates to all of the pens in hopes that Layla would enter into one of them. She did, and Corazon followed full steam ahead, determined to "set her straight." She dashed back out of the pen and ran to the corner of the pasture. Both geldings then proceeded to double-barrel her (when a horse puts their back end toward another and lifts both hind legs at the same time to kick out). She turned, with a swollen belly, and also gave an impressive high and hard double-barrel, fluid coming out of her back end as she did so.

My greatest fear was that she was going to lose her baby in the madness. Cussing at myself about my stupidity and offering unfiltered words of profanity to my herd, eventually I was able to separate her from the others. When it was time for her to have her baby, she did not give birth. Two weeks passed. I was nervous and troubled that their violent skirmish had caused damage to her and her unborn foal. Then one day, as I listened more deeply and allowed my intuition to open, I had a hunch. She still was not feeling safe, even with a horse next to her pen with a secure metal fence dividing them. I moved the horse away from her, which gave Layla a tremendous amount of space. The following morning, during a dramatic red and orange sunrise, she gave birth to a spunky bright red foal.

Layla stayed separate from the others for almost a full year. When I integrated her foal, I was also finally able to combine her without the other herd members taking issue. There were still many displays of dominance between her and my mustang. Placing Layla and Corazon together took over a year. Even though, for the most part, they got along, there was always a tension in the herd, and tempers would flare up, spats were common, and the herd was constantly moving around, either going after each other or getting out of the way.

I learned a lot about integrating horses through Layla. Some relationships require particular timing; other relationships are just not meant to happen. Clearly, what Layla needed was to be in charge of her own herd. Equally as clear was Corazon's unwillingness to allow that to happen. Eventually, I found a home for Layla with a young lady who gave her tons of attention and rode her at shows and events. Layla was very happy and became the lead mare within her new home. The day she left my ranch, a peaceful harmony, one that I had not recognized for a long time, came back to the land and the remaining herd members. We all took a big sigh of relief.

***

Esperanza, another mare, came to me years later. As a half-Friesian and half-Polish Arab, her presence was dazzling, large, excitable, and engaging. Her energy felt big and powerful, but at the same time, nervous. She had lots of questions about her new home and her new herd mates.

Esperanza stands 15.2 hands, so in physical reality, she is not a big horse. Moon, my elder, stands at 16.2. Yet, when the two of them were close by each other, Moon felt dwarfed next to her. Moving Esperanza around took a solid presence and a direct, confident, and focused handler. As a "big girl" who had received very little ground training, she tended to treat humans as she did other horses. She lacked an understanding of and respect for the personal space of others.

I wish I could say that I started working with her right away and she got integrated in no time whatsoever. The reality was that all summer I was dealing with a shoulder injury so had to integrate her at a much slower pace. Esperanza worked in programs, grazed in the fields, and slowly was let out with individual members of the herd when I deemed it to be a safe situation.

I was astonished at how eager she was to learn several of the routines of the ranch. She was always the first to come in, at full gallop, heading right back into the stall. Then she would turn and look at me with inquisitive eyes. She was more than happy to demonstrate cooperation in hopes of staying on at the ranch.

She and Corazon had still not been let out together. Every day, I watched them very closely to see when and where either of them displayed aggression. I let them eat next to each other along the fence line of their paddocks, and over time, things changed from Esperanza not daring to eat her hay at all, to her sneaking a few bites. Eventually, they began to eat peacefully next to each other, sometimes sneaking bites from each other's piles, while still separated by the metal fence. I eventually put their new slow feeding bags on the fence, and they began to eat out of the same bag.

Out of respect for my mustang's consistent wild nature of controlling the herd and any headstrong mare that came to the ranch (which ironically seemed to be *every* mare that came to the ranch), I moved slowly. I had learned my lessons, and my strong desire to have no horse hurt on my ranch shaped how I integrated Esperanza and Corazon. I took a more patient, step-by-step process to preserve the health and well-being of all of the horses on a physical and emotional level. Corazon demonstrated that his way of being in the world includes beating on new members of the herd ruthlessly and not giving in.

One day I woke with a strong feeling that it was "the day." As I walked out to the paddocks, I saw that my neighbor of six years was putting his barn sour horses out to the pasture next to mine for their very first time since I had lived next to him. My first thought was, "Bummer, I can't do it today as Corazon will go crazy with all of those new horses to meet. It would be chaos." Then, as I stopped and reflected, I realized that the truth was the exact opposite. It was a perfect time. I could utilize Corazon's strong drive for rounding up mares and protecting his herd to my advantage.

I let Corazon out of the paddock, and he was hot to trot. He immediately headed to the fence line where he and the lead mare of my neighbor's herd began a very loud conversation accented by hoof-stomping, posturing, and diving for each other's necks with white flashes of teeth. When their discussion calmed down, I then proceeded to put Esperanza out, leaving Moon in his paddock where he could watch without getting caught up in a big rowdy runaround. At twenty-eight and with arthritis, the last thing I needed was him engaged in their drama. I left Diva next to him so he would not feel wholly deserted.

Once I let Esperanza out of her paddock, she dove into the green grass near Moon's paddock. Corazon came racing across the field, and, for a split second, I doubted my actions. Did I make the wrong decision? However, he simply shooed her closer toward Moon and Diva as he turned and postured to the other herd, clearly communicating that he was the lead stallion of his herd. Corazon then ran back over to the neighbor's horses for more conversation with the lead mare. My next step was deciding to let Diva out. She was curious and ran on over with Corazon. Esperanza followed as Moon watched, ears forward and eyes bright.

After a few more minutes of noisy conversation with the neighbor's mare, Corazon turned away and herded his two females over by Moon, again posturing to the neighbor's herd. I then let Moon out and, as a herd, they began to circle in the field at a light canter. What a deliciously magical moment, seeing this colorful herd move together as one! Everyone went to say hello to the neighbor's herd and, after some more lively conversations, Corazon moved *his herd* off and to the backfield. Moon got busy herding Diva into the corner as Esperanza sheepishly hid behind Corazon.

You may be thinking, "Isn't this really just throwing them all together with a brand-new herd to meet?" The answer is no. I have learned to take specific steps before my herd is introduced to a new horse. Even with the neighbor's horses, I introduced one herd at a time to prevent a chaotic amplitude of energy, needlessly putting horses at risk of injury.

The process took five months before Esperanza was at liberty with the entire herd. The neighbor's herd functioned as a distraction to redirect Corazon's aggressive behavior. The serendipitous event resulted in an unconscious moment of protective action from Corazon. He brought Esperanza into the herd. His actions of "protecting his herd" sealed the deal with the members of my herd. He did not have the time to split the herd up to chase off the new mare aggressively. What a beautiful moment! After all of the excitement was done, I took a big breath and thought, "Everything always works out!"

So, what were the steps that helped Corazon accept this mare into the herd?

1. When she first arrived, I kept her two paddocks away from Corazon most of the time. This placement allowed space for him to observe her without the need to protect himself or other members of the herd. It also gave her time to find her grounding in her new surroundings. They could watch and size each other up. Esperanza could, at a distance, figure out the relationships that already existed in the herd.

2. Next, I started to place them next to each other in their paddocks with no feed. They could reach each other over the fencing with their heads. Many discussions ignited between them resulting in squealing and, on occasion, loud kicking on the solid metal fence that divided them.

3. Then, I began to place their piles of hay on opposite sides of their pens to create the maximum space from each other, preventing kicking and biting during eating times. They would eye each other and reposition their bodies, putting their hind ends to each other, while focusing attention on their own pile of feed. They were also split during their pasture time. The green spring grass kept them busy, and they had no desire for conversations over the fencing.

4. After a few weeks, I moved their hay closer together, while still keeping them in their separate paddocks. I placed the piles closer together each day. Soon, their personal space bubbles (about four to six feet of space around each horse) were overlapping at eating time. Eventually, their body language shifted from posturing and moving their hind ends toward each other to standing parallel with each other without any cries, pinned ears, warning snaps with their teeth, or swishing of the tails. This step took about a month.

5. I continued to move the piles closer and closer until they were practically eating out of the same pile with only a fence between them.

Again, I waited until all body language of dominance or aggression ceased before the next step.

6. Finally, I brought hanging feeding bags for both of them (because they both eat so fast) and proceeded to hang them right next to each other on the same fence line. All aggression had subsided. I knew they were close when they were both eating out of the same feeding bag.

All of these smaller steps were key. The slow approach in bringing the two horses closer together physically meant that they never felt overwhelmed, preventing them from moving into fight-or-flight and losing all sense and connection to their brain. Then, the magic of my neighbor's horses being released into the field next to my herd worked to my advantage. Corazon focused on protecting his entire herd, rather than trying to keep Esperanza away from Moon and Diva.

There are many approaches we can take in life. We can simply throw horses together and see how the dust settles—often causing unneeded pain or injury. Accidents can happen, and when they do, we experience the degree that one horse will go to keep another away. And other times, we can develop strategies. The latter requires that we become keen observers of the subtle body language of members of the herd, and we tune into timing.

Everything in life is about timing. It's about sensing the moments that are prime for a new unfolding and having the courage to take a chance and step forward into those opportunities. In these particular examples with my herd, many positive steps led to reaching the end goal.

As humans, when we stay conscious about the timing of events in our lives and listen to the messages of our heart and gut, we make choices and take actions that lead us to discoveries and integrations that may have felt impossible at one time. We want to develop strategies so we feel safe venturing into new communities of people.

Often, I see people get stuck. They fear being attacked, losing a sense of self, or being rejected. These disempowering reactions and behaviors do not have to happen. Everything is in its right timing. Which horse in the above scenarios do you relate to most? Do you tend to go to apathy and nonchalance, similar to Moon? Do you play small and stay out of the way like Diva? Are you protective and defensive like Scotch? Maybe you are like Layla, and you often try to find your way to the top or to lead so that you can hide your vulnerability. You may feel that you need to take all matters into your own hands and rightfully protect what you perceive is an external threat, often creating damage and repercussion, as Corazon does. We all have our ways of dealing with human herd dynamics.

Through the process of integration, Esperanza has shrunk (energetically speaking), or at least that is how it has appeared to me. In all actuality, the nervous energy produced in her body and mind caused by her transition into my herd has started to diminish. Her first energy center, located at the base of her spine, is where safety and trust are processed. This area was initially activated and overcharged. When she arrived, she was unsure of who she was and of her place in the herd. She was high-headed and always on the move. Slowly, she shared space with Moon and Diva and established her position with them. She became more confident and settled in her space and understanding of the ways and routine of the ranch. Her first energy center moved from expressing excessive energy based in fear and uncertainty into a more balanced, grounded energy as she developed a stronger sense of belonging.

Of course, she has not changed in physical size at all. It is the energy bubble around her, her energy field, which has changed in the quality of vibration that now gives her a different appearance. Esperanza is still 15.2 hands high. What has changed is her demeanor. She is softer now, a little bit more aware of her space and others, and more present in her body.

We have all seen this expressed in our human-to-human relationships. When a person is afraid, uncomfortable, or unsure of how they belong in a group, they will compensate by either pulling their energy in and getting smaller or by projecting their energy outward into their field, creating a static buzzing. Esperanza did the latter.

REFLECTIONS

Layla's and Esperanza's stories demonstrate that when a horse is entering into a new herd it can be tricky business. Both stories demonstrate how important it is for us to see everyone, be it a human or a horse, as an individual. The energetic expression of that individual may change, for better or worse, over time. It is no different for humans when they move and enter into new communities. Finding where one belongs takes time, but it is needed. Everyone wants to belong and find his or her herd. Our job is to experience the energy and emotion of the new member of the herd. We must assess what that energy is expressing about the individual's current state of mind and body, and then support the unfolding of the being's experience without pushing an agenda.

- Who in your life, human or horse, is currently going through tremendous change?
- What can you perceive is shifting in their energy field during this change?
- How might they benefit through your nonjudgmental observation of their process?

What Does It Mean for You?

My lovely half Friesian and half Arab gray, Esperanza, is friendly, lively, sensitive, and can have enormous energy. Her level of intelligence is often a bit shocking to me. When I speak with her, I feel no barriers. Instead, I sense her understanding and digesting what I say. She then immediately gives feedback through doing precisely the action that I have asked, without any sort of signal from my body or from any of the typical horse training tools. Esperanza has been with me for a year. She has had plenty of space and ample time to find her way within the herd. She has found her grounding and understands how to be a teaching horse for my Equine Facilitated Learning and Coaching (EFLC) program.

On a lovely day, I decided to play with her in my small arena, which is surrounded by trees and feels cozy and intimate. Initially, I intended to prepare her for a group coming in for the EFLC program, which includes developing natural horsemanship skills. We stood quietly in the arena. After stroking Esperanza's back and withers with a gentle yet firm caress, I took the halter off her head. I decided that everything we did would be at liberty. A horse at liberty has no halter on and no lead line connected to her, giving her complete freedom to respond to the environment or me as she wants to. These tools or devices are not to be used to strike a horse in any way. The two small whips I carry at times are only used to extend my energy field and area of influence. Simultaneously I used both whips, creating a little energy in each as I held them near her back end. I stood a good six-foot distance from her, and slowly we began to move around the arena. She was very willing and wanted to walk with me. As her eye gently stayed on me, she watched my arms and the whips navigate and direct her movements.

A small wooden bridge sat on top of the sand, and when we approached, she moved with softness and without hesitation over the bridge. She then approached the eight-inch-wide white PVC plumbing pipes placed on the ground, tilted upward with one end sitting on the rail of the arena panels. The objects present a visual challenge and require a horse to know precisely where they place all four of their hooves and legs. I could sense her speeding up and anxiety rising in her body. Her head got higher, and all of her muscles became tight and pulled in. She started to move faster, and her eyes became much more alert. She got spooked while walking through the poles during a past program. She had rushed through, knocking down all of the poles and frightening herself.

She needed to do it again but this time she couldn't rush through in a panic again because it would only produce the same results. I firmly raised my stick and held it in front of her and said "*slow*," requesting that she stop before getting tangled up in the pipes. She stopped and stood, her eyes looking at me with one big question: "What now?" I told her she was to move through the pipes slowly and gently. I reminded her that even though she had a bad experience running through these poles in the past, she could slow down today. I told her to pay attention to each hoof and leg and place each one very strategically. Then I let out my breath, allowing any tension in my body to release, and I lowered my stick. She proceeded forward very slowly, not once touching a single pipe with her legs. She completed walking through the eight pipes, stopped at the end, turned, and looked at me. "Well done!" I told her. I felt joyful for her success and ability to listen to me and settle her body.

Then, I guided her over to the pedestal. The pedestal is about 18 inches high. Corazon, my mustang, loves it and will immediately put his two front hooves up onto the platform. He will stand there for a long time and stretch his back while I scratch his withers. He loves being "the wild stallion on top of the mountain." As I guided Esperanza to the pedestal, I could tell she felt less confident. Remember, this entire time, she had been at liberty. I had no halter or rope that connected us and gave me any control over how she moved her body. I only had my body language and the influence of the short whips to create energy and containers, limitations, or suggestions. She had the opportunity to leave our partnership at any time she wanted to.

Once at the pedestal, I gently tapped it with a whip and asked her to place her front hooves upon it. She had no interest in looking at the big black box or in getting up on it, and moved away. I did not try to correct her but walked along beside her. We walked with her circling far away from the pedestal to the far end of the arena. I asked her with my whips to turn and face the pedestal from far away, then I asked her to return to it. She willingly did so.

This time she lowered her nose and took a good look at the big black box. Her nose reached forward and touched the box. "Well done!" I said, giving her positive feedback for her courage to try. Once again, I tapped the box with my whip, asking her to lift her hoof. With her head relaxed, her gaze came into my heart, and I felt myself soften. Then, out of the blue, I heard myself say: "What does it mean for you if you get up on this box for me?" The statement surprised me and confused me a bit. In fact, it made no logical sense. As I continued to gaze at her, she began to lick and chew, yawn, and stretch, and her head dropped very low. There was a significant shift in the energy between us. I sensed there was importance in what I said, but I was still feeling odd about why I had said it.

So, I tried to answer the question or address what I sensed were her concerns. I told her that getting up on the big black box was not something that she had to do. It was not something that would make or break our relationship. Instead, it was an opportunity for her to explore. And if she wanted once she was up, I would scratch her withers, she would stretch her back, and it would be a joyful experience. I tried to tell her that the big black box did not have to mean anything for *her*.

Again, she was at liberty. She had no halter on, and there was no lead line for me to use to guide her. She had been on the box before—however, that time, she was in a halter with a lead line. For me, a halter represents a way that a human being can guide and help a horse. It is also often how we think we can control a horse. I put myself in a position of being another horse as I strive for the most "natural" horsemanship approach. When the horse has no human-made constraints placed on her, she knows she can do what she pleases. I have only my body, arms, and voice to offer assistance or make requests. Esperanza licked and chewed with her head dropped down, fully relaxed.

I knew something significant had happened between us. And if I am entirely honest, I was still a little bit confused by the question that had come out of my mouth, feeling it spoken through me without my conscious volition. I decided one more time to ask Esperanza to get up on the big black box. I relaxed my breath and extended positive energy out to her as I gently tapped on the big black box with my whip. She moved over, lifted a leg, and placed her hoof on the pedestal. I immediately told her, "Well done, beautiful lady!" I poured vibrant, joyful energy from my heart to hers.

In reflection of my moment with Esperanza, I realized that the question that sprang from my mouth, I initially thought, was for her to answer. Now, I understand it was her question for me to answer. What did it mean for *me* to have Esperanza get up on the box? Once I shared with her that it was no big deal, and we had all of the time in the world, she relaxed. I also told her that doing it or not doing it would not change our relationship and that we were exploring and playing. Her eyes softened. She felt that I had no big agenda. She gave me what she wanted to, and I was okay with that. That was her *try*. What was most important was that I understood and saw her attempt, and I did not push her harder. If I had pushed her, I believe I would have broken our connection and understanding of each other. Her getting up on the box did not have to mean anything *for me*. My confidence as a horsewoman was not involved. My ego was not attached to success. She did not have to take the requested action to validate my skills or me.

I am confident that you have had this moment in your life. Maybe it was with another person or an animal. The pivotal moment is when a question or truth is shared that brings two people to a deeper understanding of each other. My horses are not push-button horses. They are allowed to be teaching horses, and I expect them to be a partner in the conversation. I do not endlessly ask them to do things, so they become mindless wheels in a cog, fulfilling the requirement just to please the whim of their human. If fact, if I am entirely honest, it bothers me when I see people forcing horses to go around and around in a circle, with no real interaction, while the human talks to someone else or sends text messages on their cell phone. I just don't get it.

Both Corazon and Esperanza are two horses that ask, "Why?" They each want to know the reason I ask them to do something. Esperanza is often easygoing about new things. Corazon can become downright stubborn if he does not fully understand.

The question, "What does it mean for you if I do this *for* you?" has stayed with me. It has brought me into deep ponderings about why we ask animals to do the things we ask them to do. It even extends into human-to-human relationships. We can hold significant meaning around what others do for us.

Playing in the pen with Esperanza that day gave me a tool that I've used many times to deepen my relationships with my herd members. It shed light on how to let go of attachment and help the relationship grow through trust. Both of us came away with a new understanding of the bonds between us—all by asking a simple question and allowing her to find the answer.

REFLECTIONS

Having no attachments to the actions of others can bring a particularly good sense of inner liberation. As humans, we often make personal meaning from what others do around us. When interactions with others can be fun and delightful, but not define your worth or a sense of personal power, it no longer has the hooks of codependency. You can then more easily move into the energy of amusement and dance in relationships. This dance allows you to live in the moment with grace and ease.

- Why do you ask your horse to do certain things at certain times? Who is it serving?
- What does it mean for you (and about you) when your horse does something you request?

- What happens for you when you fail to inspire your horse to action?
- What does it mean for you to influence others to new actions?
- How are you affected by your expectations of people's or animals' behaviors? What might happen if you let go of those expectations?
- What happens for you when in your human-to-human relationships, you make another's action (or non-action) hold significant meaning about your worth?

Belonging to a Herd

Typically, spring is the busiest time of year for me, and 2020 was no different; I had several spring programs filled with eager students looking forward to working with my masterful herd. My students typically come from different corners of the world, including Ireland, Dubai, South America, Canada, and Australia. Additionally, I had three corporate programs scheduled throughout the spring months with deposits already paid. All of the programs planned would bring 80 percent of my income for the year. The funds would pay for my helpers, marketing, horses, and monthly mortgage for the ranch.

By May 2020, I, like most of the world, had been on lockdown for two months. The COVID virus was shaping the lives of everyone in the world. Airlines stopped flying, stores closed, people rushed to stock up on food, and banks began to limit cash withdrawals. Like many others, big questions began to filter through my head throughout every day: What is going to happen? Will food run out? Will thousands die? Who do I trust? Will people become violent? Who knows what is happening and what our future holds? If I become sick, will I live or die?

The only option was to reschedule all of my spring programs and reorganize the many individuals who had signed up. My previously scheduled corporate programs canceled with intentions of rescheduling. All of my clients had questions about how I was going to handle the future, and the only reply I could give them was that I would know when we got there. Being in the now, staying in the present moment was the only coping strategy that seemed to work, along with getting outside to breathe fresh air and move my body.

And, as we all know, the challenge did not stop there. So many unknowns were upon the human race, and for the most part, everyone was in the same boat. Each person was having their challenges with the profound changes that suddenly occurred in their life. Ample stories of hardship emerged every day, so there was no shortage of ways to compare my life to others and to feel lucky that I was on my land with trees, green grass, room to move and breathe, and to be with my horses. However, the financial responsibility of my herd, the land, and employees weighed heavily on me. The only solution I could find to raise funds was to launch programs online so people could work with me from their homes. Luckily for me, people signed up, and I made enough money for a few months.

Initially, I thought I would have plenty of extra time to enjoy life, breathe a bit, and for the first time in all my years of teaching, have the spring season off. The opposite proved true. The pressures to keep the few part-time employees I had and to keep my ranch pushed me hard. I launched even more programs. Gradually, the limitations on society lifted, but it did not lift concerns from my students. It had become a fearful and frustrating time for everyone.

The truth was, I had been struggling with health issues for a few months, and the possibility of surgery loomed overhead. Was I ready to have ten people on my property, bringing their lives, energy, and any noxious germs into my environment? Was I comfortable with them touching so much of my belongings and my beloved horses? Could I trust that all of the students who would come were also practicing social distancing?

And, what if something happened? Could I live with the realization that people got sick because I kept a program on the calendar? After much thought, I decided to cancel all spring programs and move the equine educational programs online. Now I had to make videos, find individuals who could be my models, record classes, and more. Technology has never been intuitive for me. I, like many others, was stretched to the limit, pushed into imbalance. Several times, I woke in the morning with an overwhelming sensation of wanting to throw up. Certainly, this was no way to live. The stress of it all took a toll on my well-being.

Internally, I was embarrassed. Teaching others to reach higher levels of emotional intelligence and spiritual concepts, yet not taking care of myself as I desperately needed to, made me a hypocrite. That was not working for me. I declared that moving forward, I would commit to my daily self-care including long walks, bike rides, yoga, playing with my horses, gardening, or artwork. I needed to get my mind off the fear and anxiety present in the world.

Spring was cool, with snow and hailstorms in between warm sunny days. Tree buds were hesitant to reemerge after being previously pelted. The songs of the birds were alive and boisterous. The pastures turned green overnight, and peace prevailed within the confines of my six acres. The horses found lots of mud puddles to roll in, helping to clump up and pull the winter coats off their body. They adored being groomed and lined up to wait their turn. Corazon, my mustang, always pushes the others aside so he can be the first to receive affection and attention. The more sugar-filled fresh green grass they ate, the happier they became. I wonder if they thought it odd that no people arrived at the ranch this spring. They enjoyed the sun getting warmer and the grass getting taller and sweeter to eat each day as time passed.

One day, after feeling stressed out the day before, I decided to drop everything and spend the entire afternoon on my beautiful small ranch. Buds on the trees were finally pushing up and outward. Perennials were sprouting, and the irises started to show their true colors. What the heck was I doing in the house working like a slave? Moon, my elderly buckskin horse, takes a very long time to lose his winter coat completely. He hangs on to it like a well-worn shirt that is soft and cozy. Then, as the days get warmer, he will suddenly be ready for all of the hair to be groomed off. It is thick and fine-haired, often two inches deep, with each layer bringing a different color to the surface as it comes off. The process of getting to his summer coat can take hours in a day and many weeks in the process. He, of course, is happy as a clam. Compared to the other herd members, Moon receives the most grooming time and attention.

Moon's mane was a mess. Two rainstorms and lots of rolling out in the field had left him with eight-inch thick dreadlocks. I had my job cut out for me. We stood by ourselves in a paddock with Corazon in the paddock just next to us. As I groomed Moon near the fence, Corazon found his way over. There he stood, intently staring at me. He watched my every move as I hummed a lovely song and stood in deep harmony with Moon. Moon's head got heavy, and his eyelids drooped; he was falling asleep. Very gently and without pulling, I untangled his entire mane. Gobs of blackballed hair surrounded me on the ground, along with many shades of caramel-colored tufts from his body. He was now truly a buckskin in transition, looking similar to a patchwork quilt of many colors. He and I stood together with our feet solidly on the earth, thinking about nothing but the moment. Then Corazon began to paw the ground. He was letting me know that he would be next.

Without leaving Moon's pen, I simply reached over the fence and began to scratch Corazon's withers. Unlike Moon, his coat was gone entirely. A subtle shine was starting to emerge, and before long, he would be a specimen of vibrant health. However, just like Moon, his black mane was all bunched up into thick dreadlocks. Typically for Corazon, he dislikes all spray bottles, and he usually walks away. I always groom my horses at liberty and give them the option to walk away. I kept humming and scratching and told him I needed to apply a little detangler spray. I thought for sure he would leave as he had done for the entire ten years of our relationship. I often thought he was just too proud to accept that level of grooming; after all, he was a wild horse. A wild horse does not go to a beauty parlor.

On this day, he stood still and unphased by any of my movements. Even as I held the squirt bottle behind and above his head he stayed still. Then, I sprayed copious amounts of detangler into his mane. As it ran down his neck, he still did not move. Ever so gently, I began to work on his dreadlocks. He continued to be still. I decided to move to his side of the fence. He walked over to the gate to affirm that I still intended to finish the job I had started. I squirted more conditioner on his massively matted black hair and sat the plastic bottle on the ground. Eventually, he crept toward the bottle. Slowly his head lowered, and he began to play with the bottle. Really? Who was this horse, and what did he do with my wild mustang?

After I finished his mane, Corazon insisted that I scratch him all over. He moved his shoulder toward me, then took a step forward so I could touch his back. I pressed in hard with my nails around his withers, digging in deeply. His head raised, and his lips began to scrunch up as he exposed his white teeth. He reached his head around to show me his expression, so I would not miss the great pleasure I was bestowing upon him. His funny-looking face made me laugh out loud. Then finally, I stopped. There I stood, and he stood quietly beside me. Moon, still on the other side of the fence, stood calmly and quietly. I allowed my breath to deepen into my body even further. I paused to reflect.

That is when I felt a sense of emotion move through my body. Days of suppressing my stress and fears had left me tightly wound. Grooming my horses had shifted the tightness, and my nervous system started to release and reset. Gentle tears streaked my face as I realized that as much as I can handle being by myself, living alone during COVID was a challenge. Being with my herd and grooming them, having them touch me with their nose and lean on me, filled me with the healing energy of touch. We all need physical contact and touch, and I'd had none for two months.

Looking deeply into Corazon's steady, reliable eyes, I expressed my gratitude for his offering and for being in my life. I reflected on where we were ten years earlier when he seldom wanted to be touched, untrusting of humans and their intentions. He stood without the man-made halter around his head, and I, with my COVID mask hanging around my neck. In that moment, I realized that COVID for humans felt similar to what it feels like for a wild horse when captured. One day, life is going along as usual. The horse is in their daily routine; they have bonds with their wild family or herd and trust their relationships. They have a sense of what to anticipate as the day moves forward. But then, suddenly, chaos descends, forever changing what one knows as normal.

Corazon was ripped from his family and placed into a human-made metal trailer. He then was hauled away from wild lands he had lived on his entire life, never to return. He also experienced several different environments before finally arriving at the prison in Colorado, where an inmate would gentle him. There he was made to get used to wearing a halter around his head. The questions he had during his transition must have been similar to the questions humans had during the first COVID outbreak. What is going to happen? Will food run out? Where is my family? Are they alive? Who do I trust? Will people become violent? Who knows what is happening and what my future holds? Will I die? How can I find my way back? And, will I ever run free again?

Change is the only constant, and life is transforming at all times. Times of drastic and dramatic change call for high levels of adaptability. Corazon is living proof of the skill and ability. Corazon had no choice but to accept the circumstances of a dramatic life change and to find himself in the hands of a woman who knew little to nothing about training a wild horse.

Corazon mourned the loss of a life once known so he could find acceptance in a new life that was forced upon him. He had to accept that his natural, wild nature would eventually become tempered and domesticated. He ultimately would find trust in the world of man and know that he would embrace the unfolding of each day, just as he had in the wild. Corazon was once standoffish and untrusting. Now, he readily told me where he would like his scratches.

As I looked at him thinking about his process of adaptation, I thought: *Beautiful wild horse, if you can do what you did, certainly I can get through COVID.* I realized that I must honor that I have already creatively begun a path of adaptability. Stress is a part of changes that transpire through transition and trauma, and finding more acceptance and pacing ourselves can bring more balance and less stress. Most of all, we must remember who we are, at our core, and to find an inner strength to adapt in a way that supports a new journey, one unexpected, and possibly more vibrant and more rewarding. In a world that has already changed, we must trust that a day will come when things will be relaxed again, and we all will have the comfort of human connection and touch.

In the meantime, I embrace that I belong to this herd. I walk on the land with them, I read and meditate with them. I feed and groom them. When in the round pen, we flow together in synchronistic co-creation as equals. These lovely four horses are creatures of kindness and internal harmony. They have accepted me as one of them, not just a person that demands things of them. So that day, as the two large hawks brought twigs to build a new nest high up in the old grandfather cottonwood tree, I stood below it, being one with my herd, knowing that all would change and eventually a new day would emerge.

REFLECTIONS

The COVID virus has caused us to take a deep look at personal and systemic changes in all parts of life. The fallout has ripped us from what we once knew, with no clear sight of what the new normal will be. Like Corazon, time will help us adjust and allow us to find a place in our new reality. Although we need social distancing and often isolation for an unknown time, the relationships we have up close and at a distance will be even more important. Belonging to a herd is an important part of the human experience. To help you navigate the way forward, get your journal out and write about the following questions:

- How do you adapt to the change the world is requiring?
- Do you look outside or inside of yourself to find comfort?
- Where and how do you source the feeling of true connection? Can you find that in nature? Can you find it

with an animal, listening to the birds, or appreciating the beauty of flowers and trees?

- What helps you keep your balance and harmony, unaffected by the stresses of the unknowns in the world?

Equine Bathing with Diva

There is a first for everything, and I was beside myself to be going on my first-ever horse camping trip. My lovely mare, Diva, would accompany me. We had been riding the local trails all spring, and we were both physically fit and ready to go. I could hardly wait.

I spent an entire day packing all of the vital pieces to ensure a perfect trip. Pat, the woman I'd be riding and camping with, had given me a complete list. The only thing I did not have was a pair of barefoot shoes. They are very expensive, and I had never used them.

Pat and I loaded the trailer and made the three-hour drive into the Rocky Mountains of Colorado, where we would set up camp in campgrounds that had corrals for the horses. All we had to do was maintain the grounds and haul water, manure, and feed. Arriving in the early afternoon, we decided to go for a short scouting ride before the third camper, Sue-Anne, who I did not know, joined us.

Pat and I enjoyed a lovely, albeit short ride from the campsite. The tall pine trees provided ample shade, and the trail moved in and out of small pale green fields dotted with late July wildflowers. When we returned, I untacked Diva. As I groomed her, I saw that she was missing a shoe. Darn! That was not good. It must have just happened on the return, and I was surprised I did not notice it.

I looked all around the campsite and even walked the trail we had been on but was unable to find it. I was there to ride and had put a tremendous amount of energy into the preparations needed to get us both to the campsite, including securing a house sitter to tend to the rest of my herd and my high-strung wired-hair Jack Russell.

We immediately began to try to figure out what solutions might work. I explored the concept of making a shoe. If I could find the materials, I had plenty of duct tape. I could wrap something to make a lift for my mare's hoof. I sat with Diva and prepared a go-to replacement shoe, cutting out cardboard, fitting it to her foot, and arduously cutting more cardboard pieces. Sitting next to her outdoor stall, I began to tape it all together.

Diva is such a sweet mare. She stood patiently, watching me with curiosity as I wrapped and wrapped. I knew it was probably a long shot since she weighed about 1,000 pounds. Duct tape is reliable, but the layers of cardboard would likely quickly break down. But it was my only option if I wanted to ride. The closest farrier was two-and-a-half hours away, so I sat for a good hour with Diva, preparing her new shoe. Of course, Pat was a bit upset because if I could not ride my horse, it would create organizational challenges and conflict. Typically, you do not leave one horse behind. When you camp with people and horses, the whole herd goes together on the journey.

Feeling the tension in the air, I worked even harder to figure out a solution. It became the afternoon project for me. I was very diligent and quite proud of myself when eventually I had a pad thick enough to duct-tape to Diva's foot. I took her out for a little walk around the campground to see how well it would work out, and as you've likely guessed, it was pretty much a joke. Within minutes, even though there were layers of duct tape to hold it in place, my handmade shoe frayed and came off.

Now I was starting to get stressed. The last thing I wanted was to upset others in the group. I could tell Pat was worried I would not be able to ride. After a while, she said maybe she could look in her trailer and find a barefoot shoe. She came out with a shoe that fit my mare. Diva accepted it, although she was still a bit uneven. Continuing to be creative, I took the handmade shoe and inserted it into the barefoot clog. We tried one more time with Diva, and with that, she stood still and was perfectly balanced. She moved with no problem or any hesitation and never lifted her foot again. I put her saddle on her and rode her around a bit. She was comfortable, and I was thrilled to be back in the game. I let out a big sigh of relief. I would not end up disappointing others.

Additionally, I felt the entire process brought Diva and me closer. We sat together for some time while I had worked the cardboard and tape together. I watched her watch me. I would simply ask her to lift her foot by putting one finger on her leg, and she would. Near the end, I would simply say, "Okay, Diva, give me your hoof now." She would then raise it for me so I could make more adjustments. In the process of solving the missing shoe, she and I had dropped into conversation and connection.

A few hours later, Sue-Anne arrived. Pat helped her unload her horse and put him in the stall. Then we all hung out near the campfire and had dinner. Pat began to tell us about where we were riding the next day. There was a lovely little river crossing in a ravine that was supposed to be a bit of a challenge, and I hadn't done a lot of water crossings with Diva, so I was raring to go. We had solved the problem with her shoe by combining my pad into a barefoot shoe that Pat found in her tack room. I was bound and determined that Diva and I would not only ride but also get across the water.

Sue-Anne then informed us that she wasn't planning on riding her horse on this particular camping trip because she did not feel confident riding in the woods. If you could have seen Pat's face, her mouth dropped nearly to the ground. Pat drilled Sue-Anne, asking why, if she had come on this camping trip for riding with horses, she would not be going out on the trail? I sat on the sidelines, wondering how this was going to work out, trying to be patient while realizing I'd be hanging out with these women for the next three days.

Long story short, nothing got resolved, and we all went to bed. The next morning, we woke to frost on our tents and the horses moving around trying to warm up. We immediately put hay down, realizing that the temperatures had dropped into the low thirties overnight. Unfortunately, Pat's horse was showing signs of colic. Her mare was having a tough time handling the change in elevation and the cold temperatures. We administered both Banamine and electrolytes, and her mare drank some water. An hour later, she started to eat. We all sighed in relief.

Now, we had to sort out what we were going to do for the ride. As you can imagine, horse camping with someone who didn't want to ride was an odd adventure. We certainly could not leave Sue-Anne and her horse alone at camp. The horses had been together overnight, and her horse skills were not very proficient. So, we compromised. On the first day, we went out to one of the fields and practiced ground skills around fallen logs and other natural obstacles. Playing with our horses was fun. However, Pat and I were still keen to ride.

The next day, I suggested that if we weren't going to ride, at least we could get our horses down to the river to practice some water crossings. Sue-Anne could tag along and do whatever she wanted with her horse. So, off we went, Pat's horse and mine saddled, allowing us a combination of walking our horses and then a little bit of riding. Along the way, we would frequently ride back to check on Sue-Anne, who was only walking her horse.

The excursion turned out to be enjoyable. I liked hiking along with Diva on a single track. I could hear her hoofs striking the ground behind me. I found a rhythm with Diva as we navigated through the woods and the pastures. When we traversed through muddy areas, I would jog with her beside me in a trot on the extensive trails up the hillsides. She and I were in tune with each other. The farther we went into the forest, the more in tune I was with all of nature. Being by my horse's side instead of in the saddle created an entirely different conversation. I found it to be great fun.

We went along a rocky section of the trail with a significant drop-off to the left. I kept a fair distance from my mare, reminding Diva, with a wave of my lead line, not to come on top of me. The others did the same with their horses. Both mentioned how they had walked with their horses but had never hiked in the woods on the varied rocky terrain we were on. We all agreed that it was taking a bit of focus to make sure our horses did not encroach upon our space, as they might do with each other in their nature herds. Maintaining that space and not getting stepped on, or worse, be run over if the horse should spook, was critical, especially in the rocky territories.

Then, we came down into a moist area where bright green grass covered the soggy ground. We had entered into a micro-ecosystem. Surrounded by the dry, rock-filled terrain, this gentle alcove near the river seemed out of place with its emerald foliage growing beneath the clear water. The moisture hit my skin, cooling my body down from the sun's heat. Diva and I had already crossed other boggy areas, and she offered no hesitation at this spot. She followed me to the river's small, sandy edge. The distance to the opposite side of the river where we stood was about sixty feet with a thigh-deep depth. The edges of the river were clear and calm, but you could see the center had larger rocks, and the current produced enough white froth that made seeing the bottom of the river difficult in those areas.

There was a sweetness to the section of the river where we would cross. The green vegetation above and around us formed a canopy, creating an enveloping feeling of safety, comfort, and calmness. The setting was magical and almost mystical. As we stood next to the stream, Pat started giving Sue-Anne a lesson on how to get her horse to place his hooves into the water. They stood at an area that had a small pool and was perfect for this practice. Diva and I moved around the brush and down the river a bit.

I stood with Diva and watched her head rise, her eyes becoming alert. Her nostrils opened up as she took in the fragrance of fresh water rolling over rocks, and the bright, moist growth that contrasted the typical drier grasses found in meadows midsummer. Her senses opened, and as her ears perked forward, I could tell she was listening to everything. My hearing also expanded as I listened to the water gently but very lively moving on its course. I could hear the chirping birds in the trees above, the crickets and frogs in the grass, and the voices of my new friends. Water moving here and there over rocks or against the edge of the banks completed the living orchestra that set the tone of the moment. The moisture was intensely pleasurable, especially after hiking in the hot summer sun.

If you told me fairies lived in this green spot with crystal clear water, a slight dampness in the air, and moss on the banks' sides, I would have believed you. There was something special and unique about how the water pooled on the edges but cascaded through the center. As I stood with Diva, that specialness only increased for me. I could sense the earthly smells of all the different living creatures and flora growing on the banks. The moisture from the water seeped into my skin and nostrils.

At that moment, my breath also began to deepen. As I watched Diva, I could sense her excitement. I could feel her body absorbing all of the stimulation surrounding us. I knew more than anything that she and I would cross the riverbed, the farthest distance through moving water we'd gone together to this point.

So, while Pat and Sue-Anne continued to work in the shallow pool, I checked Diva's girth, found a rock to use as my mounting block, and climbed on. I took her to the edge of the riverbank where she put her foot in the beautiful, clear water. Once all four hooves were in the water, Diva paused. I knew there were two options at this point: I could tell Diva to back out, or gently tell her it's okay, focus on the other side of the waterway, and give her a little bit of reins and a little leg. That's what I did, and I could feel her body pulsing under me. I could feel her strength moving us through the water as it splashed up around me, soaking my boots. The water parted at her chest as we went right through. Cold and stimulated, we arrived at the other bank. Diva shook, and I could feel the excitement moving through her body, the cold water invigorating her blood. The energy buzzed through my body, and my adrenaline shot up as I laughed out loud.

In those moments of moving across that river, I gave everything of myself to my horse. I gave Diva the reins and my trust; I went for the ride. Diva did not let me down. She plowed through the water sure-footed and robust as the cold mountain water splashed on my thighs and soaked my boots. There was absolutely nothing else at that moment except my horse and me, one in nature.

I felt joyous on the other side of the river as she pranced around. Having not experienced a lot of horses with lively high energy before, I found it quite exciting. I felt comfortable because I trusted this mare so much. We turned around and saw that Pat and Sue-Anne were still on the other side of the river working with Sue-Anne's horse. They were partially hidden behind a bush. So I decided, heck, we'd just go right back across the river to them.

Feeling the oneness with nature and with Diva was so pleasurable. I could have quickly joined the women's conversation. But I knew that the entire trip was going to be different than I had imagined, and this was my lone opportunity to come into oneness with my horse to do something I'd hoped we'd do. I wanted that moment, and I went for it. We had crossed the clear waterway without fuss. She and I were both electrified with energy and joy.

Pat was ready to cross now, and her horse was giving her a great deal of resistance. When I crossed back over, I offered to have her follow my horse. Diva and I turned back around, and the two mares crossed together. Pat and I both felt that at least we'd faced a challenge on the trip and had accomplished something with our horses. The trip was not what we expected, yet some lovely pieces had come together. Her horse was okay, we got to play in the water, and Sue-Anne learned some new beautiful tactics about leading a horse in the wilderness. I also developed a deeper relationship with my horse as we spent time problem solving and just hanging out.

This camping trip taught me so much about having complete clarity when deciding to go on a journey with my horse and other people. It also taught me how the highest flexibility needs to happen whenever you want to do something with horses. One can learn from the delightful moments with their horse. They can take away from the humanness and the train-ing methods and conflicts and get into nature, just as I had with Diva. We dropped into the energy of the moment, into what that environment had to offer us. The moment wasn't just about getting across the river with Diva; it was about feeling all of the stimulation of nature. It was about hearing everything, feeling everything, and then surrendering the control to my mare and becoming one with her as we crossed that river.

The moment was delicious. As I write this, it brings tears to my eyes because I long for it again. I yearn for the tranquility and magic of the hobbit-like setting. Diva had given me the gift of entering into the water-way, being part of it all, and not being separate. For that, I will be forever grateful to her. The next year I returned to the campground with my mare. Diva and I crossed the river again, this time with two men and their geldings. It was fun, but it wasn't the same. There had been some-thing dreamlike and enchanting about that first time. And maybe it was because it was the first time.

As we stood at the bank that first trip, taking in all of the sounds and scents, Diva and I were in sync not only with the task but with the entire environment. All of nature moved through me as I listened to the spirit of my horse and witnessed the elements of nature move through her. I courageously grabbed the moment, which I will remember forever.

About a week after that first horse camping adventure, I came across a phrase forest bathing, or *shinrin-yoku*, a term meaning "taking in the forest atmosphere." First developed in Japan in the 1980s, forest bath-ing has since become a crucial part of Japanese medicine's preventative health care practices. There is a plethora of positive mental and physi-cal results from being in the forest and taking in the atmosphere (versus conquering). Forest bathing can include practices of releasing the ego's desires, breathing in the scents that are present, and feeling one's body and emotions. It can also help create a broader sense of aliveness through the entire body and allow one to focus on the present moment, giving the mind a rest from the stresses of today's world.

A broad smile came across my face as I read about forest bathing. I recognized that *shinrin-yoku* is what I had experienced with Diva the first time we crossed the river; we had entered into a lovely sacred spot in the forest, and we took it in through all of our senses. Beyond that, I had also allowed myself to take my horse in fully. I bathed in her energy as we crossed the stream. When I read the forest bathing description, I realized this was an action in which I had long ago based my philosophy of working with horses. I attempt to honor the horse and find a way to understand their world and how they are an intrinsic part of nature.

Even though I was riding Diva for my pleasure, she and I went beyond just a ride for riding's sake. We found a sweet moment together under the green canopy and the gently moving water at the river's edge. I entered into her world and gave myself over to her. She trusted me and led me across an unfamiliar obstacle. We had become one entity, wholly in the moment. This exchange of energy, the bathing in one's senses and being completely present in the moment, is much like the sessions I offer in my work—a horse and human interact, with the horse as the teacher. The horse mirrors and offers its wisdom. I guide the human to enter the world of sensory awareness and be fully present in their body. Horses create a powerful healing space and bring the human into a deep connection with self with an expanded self-awareness that includes connecting to the environment.

Although I call the work I do "coaching with horses," this unique process and exploration with horses could be called "equine bathing." This practice of being with horses on their terms, senses wide open, noticing what is arising in one's physical body, and taking in the environment through sensations allows humans to fully integrate into the horse's way. When a person is more rooted in the present moment with a gentle, kind equine friend next to them, they become one with nature again.

Mental, emotional, and physical benefits for individuals practicing the art of being with horses in the horse's way, not the human approach, are similar to those of forest bathing. There is a deep sense of coming home to the self and the connection with nature and something more significant than our body. John Muir, known as the father of the National Parks, wrote in the 1800s, "Thousands of tired, nerve-shaken, over-civilized people are beginning to find out that going to the mountains is going home. Wilderness is a necessity." I propose that thousands of stressed out, overstimulated, ungrounded, and emotionally fractured people will find their way to animals, both domesticated and wild, as a source of returning to nature in an attempt to come home. Often better medicine than pills, despite the daily risk in man's hands, nature is our true home. Animals in nature model for us a natural, biological way to be in the world. Horses, as sentient beings with high intelligence, guide us there, often when we least expect it.

We experience communion with nature when we release the need to consume property, products, information, and each other. This connection with all parts of nature is achieved when we move toward a much broader view of reality that includes respect and compassion for all living systems. To reach this understanding, we must, in essence, "rewild" ourselves by returning to what is most natural and authentic, by bathing in and inviting deep awareness as we are immersed in nature and with her creatures. Remember, we are one of her animals, too.

REFLECTIONS

- When is the last time you traveled with your equine friend? How did you deepen your relationship?
- What does it mean to be in a herd, consisting of both humans and horses? When do you want to break away, and when do you contribute?
- When did you feel closest to your horse? What were the events that led up to that moment?
- How often do you open your senses freely like your horse? Do you find those special moments on your rides, or does human conversation distract you?

PART II
Healing with Horses

Four Ways Horses Are Healers

Horses are the most excellent teachers for humans regarding healing and understanding energy fields. In a natural setting, horses are fully grounded on Mother Earth. They are, for the most part, energetically open beings. They sense the energy of the environment and the intention within the animals that are around them. The ability to read, engage, and move energy within themselves and others comes second nature to a horse. Many horses become masters at intentionally moving energy in their environment. Other horses may not reach such levels of mastery and continue to be reactive, unaware, or unproductive in their use of energy. In doing so, they remain at a lower ranking within the herd than those horses who have developed emotional and energetic mastery.

In my Coaching with Horses programs, and those around the world, horses have stepped up to be our teachers, guides, space holders, and healers for human beings of all types. Through the last fifteen years of facilitating this unique and profound work, I have watched hundreds of horses closely and have been fascinated by their responses and movements. Many of the horses show up in a way that I least expect, and show a side of their personality that often shocks their owners. The horses have full liberty to be the horse they were born to be, which is sometimes the opposite of what their owners see. In this work, horses can be authentically themselves, releasing all of the conditioning and conforming that is typically expected from them when they are with humans. As I hold space and facilitate a person through their experience with a horse, I also notice the subtleties of communication and energy exchange between the horse and a human. I am always amazed at the patterns I see and how the horses are participating in helping to shift energetic or emotional patterns held in the consciousness of the human.

My students often ask me, what are the horses doing with the energy we are offering them? What can we learn about ourselves and our energy field during this process? Why are horses so willing to be the conduit of change for humans? There are many ways that horses work with us and help us see our energetic contribution (the current energy we are offering others). Without an understanding of who we are at an emotional and energetic level and how to master agility within our energy field, we can become much like a horse who never matures enough to be trusted or given a job that requires grounding and presence. Without knowing ourselves at an intimate level, we lack the ability to allow our real soul's calling to emerge and to feel we are living the life we were born to live.

After studying horses for years, I've found four common ways that they work with our energy field and how we might better understand their nature and also the collective teachings they are bestowing upon us. The horse, as an open vessel or what I call an "acoustical being" (a being of sound and light waves), receives every aspect of our energy, including our mind, emotions, and intentions, both conscious and unconscious. What are the unique ways that they respond to and work with what we are offering them? The four common ways are horse as mirror, horse as sponge, horse as diffuser, and horse as spiritual alchemist.

HORSE AS MIRROR

If you have engaged with horses before, most certainly you have experienced the power of "horse as mirror." The horse as mirror is a widespread concept in the equine facilitated learning field of work and takes place when the horse responds to what the human offers energetically and at all levels of consciousness. The human's energy shows up through a clear expression in their body, and the horse responds to it. If we are feeling lonely and rejected, the horse moves away and affirms the deep-seated belief of our unworthiness. The movement is subtle, but the message and reflection powerful.

When we feel frustrated, fearful, and anxious, the horse brings that energy into their body and begins to move around, paw the ground, trot, or if it escalates, move into a canter. The horse goes into an energetic resonance with the human's emotions, just as they would with other horses in a herd. The horse does not consider a different behavior. Instead, the horse mirrors what is being offered by the human back to that human. A skilled coach knows how to work with the horse to help them modulate their emotions and bring their energy into check. The coach also is skilled in bringing themselves into emotional congruence and overall coherence in the heart and body. As the emotional energy becomes more contained, it prevents the energy within the horse from potentially escalating even further, causing unneeded displays of anxiousness, anxiety, fear, or worry.

The mirroring effect is powerful and can be stunning or jarring. However, the horse is revealing an unconscious aspect of the human. It is the human's choice to embrace the offering from the horse. If they awaken to the messages, better decisions can be made on an emotional, spiritual, and mental level. Whenever we are working with animals, it behooves us to ask, what is this animal mirroring back to me about my mood, emotional state of consciousness, and energy? What is this animal showing me about myself? When the animal is a mirror, it projects back to the human the energetic content of the human.

HORSE AS SPONGE

A second way a horse works with the mood or emotion that a human offers them is by becoming an energetic sponge. I have seen this very often in situations where horses feel it is their purpose or agreement to take on the energy of others, to be the healer, or to fulfill a job or purpose within their environment. The horse will embrace the human energetically and begin to take on the human's uncomfortable energy patterns so that the human may feel better. I call this concept "horse as sponge." Often, this will happen when emotions such as sadness, grief, hopelessness, and a lack of confidence arise in the human.

The human, who may or may not be in touch with the energy of their body, could leave not knowing what transpired during their time with the horse. However, they *generally* feel better. The horse is merely trying to be of service, but the sponging effect can become very detrimental to the horse's well-being if they aren't taught how to move energy productively. Horses often pick up this way of processing energy through the example that their human counterparts are unconsciously modeling. When a horse becomes a sponge, they take energy from the human's energy field into their body, and it can become stuck. They are caretaking at a very high degree. Ultimately, we want to remind and teach domesticated horses how to naturally run unwanted energy through their bodies to ground and release what they have picked up from others. These horses need a lot of movement and freedom and are best used less than the horses who are mirrors.

HORSE AS DIFFUSER

There is also the dynamic of "horse as diffuser." The horse as diffuser is a little more masterful at managing their energy than the horse as sponge. As the diffuser of energy, the horse is very clear about its own space and how to manage or "run" their energy to maintain their stance, energy bubble, and powerful healing heart. These horses are often the "glue" in the herd. They are the peacemakers and peacekeepers. They are usually in the background and do not require a lot of recognition for their contributions. The human that experiences the horse as diffuser may feel rising emotions alter and subside. The horse, more than likely, is watching purposefully, licking and chewing and letting the energy move through. The horse may be active or standing.

A shift will happen in the energy field of the human, and they often feel uplifted, more hopeful, and open. Calmness prevails over the confusion, frustration, or anger they felt at the beginning. The horse that is the diffuser feels no need to rescue the human but instead is a master at holding space and witnessing the human's process. The diffuser becomes a gentle conduit for release and change for those around them. This horse powerfully allows the energy that the human is offering to be present, and then gracefully enables the energy to flow once the human has reached a nonresistant state.

HORSE AS SPIRITUAL ALCHEMIST

Horse as spiritual alchemist is when the horse changes the energetic patterns of another. The human can experience a shift that lasts forever, removing all traces of what was, and a new, better present reality is created. These horses are masterful energetic healers that can hold space for another's process and actively help to release and transmute unproductive energy patterns or cycles.

The horse as spiritual alchemist focuses on the transmutation of something into a superior form. The horse who is the spiritual alchemist helps to awaken consciousness and most often does so in the most subtle of ways. The human often feels altered in an indescribable way. They lack the words, thought process, or ability to articulate what happened. During the process, there can be a sense of timelessness in the environment. Often at my ranch, additional environmental components play out as well, such as flocks of birds perched on tree limbs offering their orchestra of song, a silence of human activity, or a sense of stillness in the air. Additionally, the rest of my herd will stand by and watch. The horses lick and chew as the session transpires, contributing the power of their presence to the session. Experiencing a horse as spiritual alchemist can be a mystical, life-changing journey because it goes deep into a cellular level.

REFLECTIONS

Horses are powerful healers, each in their own way. As each horse grows in their work as healer, they find their level of ability. Many evolve themselves as they work with humans, transforming the participant's and their own lives. In all cases, horses and humans change in fundamental and profound ways.

- Have you ever considered why you feel better when you are with horses?
- Do you ever experience an energetic weight being lifted after you spend time with them?
- If you have horses in your life, which healing type do you observe them being?
- If you were a healer, which of the four types would you be?

The Dynamics of Energy
and Separation

The energy and concept of push and pull, in and out, touch and release, contact and disconnect, and all the cycles of inner relationship dynamics were streaming through my consciousness before one of my Equine Facilitated Learning and Coaching (EFLC) programs began in April. I had a herd of six, including a barely trained mare with a strong matriarch drive, a once wild stallion with his instinctual drive, and four additional and more domesticated herd members. Each day, I observed their cohesiveness, protection, and affection with one another, or sometimes their less affectionate and borderline aggressive behavior toward each other. This dance of self in relationship to others, the sense of oneness and safety within the herd directly contrasting the needs of each individual within that herd, creates a complex system. One that is often changing, sometimes stabilizing, and other times rearranging.

I have been on my spiritual journey now for twenty-four years, and my journey with Moon, a beautiful, dapple buckskin standing 16.2 hands high, for the last twelve years. Moon has been my rock, keeping me steadfast in the most challenging job I have ever decided to embrace—teaching others to raise their consciousness through engaging with Horse. Moon has soft, beautiful, almond-shaped soulful eyes with big broad shoulders and a large, powerful head. His mane, tail, and socks on his lower legs are black, making a stunning contrast to his caramel-colored body. He holds a heart of gold within his massive chest.

We have been doing our intimate and sometimes (for me) frustrating dance of a relationship for many years. Moon knows so clearly who he is and what he stands for. I watch him pull the other horses closer to stand in peace, or stand above protecting the yearling while she sleeps, or, in contrast, give the others "the look" so that they come no closer than about five feet into his bubble. Without attachment, he respects what he needs for his space within each moment.

When Moon first came into my life, the days he indicated to me he needed his space were the hardest. For me, his big heart, warm chest, soft eyes, and total presence were a haven against the incongruences I experienced within the public barn in which I had first placed him. When he gave me his look and walked away, I was often sad and felt pain, as all I wanted was to connect.

Some of the most profound teachings we receive come with great pain. The pain is the gateway. Pain is an opening, like a side channel of a river taking us on a different journey. We enter into places never experienced before. We always have a choice to engage our courage and to make the journey, to receive the gift, without judgment of the other, or engage with self-loathing or deprecating thoughts, creating a victim or martyr response. What we do with the information that other beings around us show us is our choice.

In all of my years with Moon, I have experienced the duality of connection and disconnect, the push and pull, and the give-and-take. Moon has taught me how to deeply connect with him at a soul level, and to also embrace the often separateness of our physical beings. He already understood that dynamic, and with his wisdom and truth, he has offered it up to me, over and over. Now, even when he chooses the distance, it is evident in my heart we are One. And then, there are those times when Moon chooses and asks for the closeness—for the touch, comfort, or connection of our physical beings. And these times, of course, for me, are the most delicious. Sitting with Moon, being with Moon, either to just be, or to care for his now aching joints, transports me to a deep well of peace and calm.

During the April program, I felt his presence calling for me while I sat with my group in the indoor meeting space. The sense I received from him was to go out and be with him. Not entirely sure of what we would do, I decided to offer the group some ideas on how to care for their "teaching horses." As we entered into the paddock, Moon was there with Ginger, a calm, intelligent filly. Her body is growing like a bean sprout in juxtaposition to her wise soul. Ginger has been watching the EFLC work from a distance since birth just over a year previously.

I asked the group to form a half-circle around Moon and Ginger. I watched to see what Ginger and Moon might decide to offer. Moon stood quietly still while, to my surprise, Ginger stepped forward. She greeted each student by placing her head on their shoulder, embracing them, and offering her pure, innocent heart for them to receive. This gesture struck me because it is much like how a mare will mother and nurture her foals.

Ginger chose when to move along to the next student and create a new soft and sweet connection. She moved, one by one, down the line of waiting ladies. The group relished the purity of Ginger's energy and the maturity and gentleness of her approach. Sometimes she would place her soft muzzle on a person's chest. A few times, Ginger placed her head on their shoulder or near their throat. Once, she used her head and nudged the student to take a step toward her. Ginger then wrapped her head around the student, placing her muzzle on her back behind her heart.

One of the participants loved the connection with Ginger so much that she snuck away from her place in the line. She then moved to the end of the line so she could connect once again with Ginger. When Ginger reached her, she looked at her for a moment and then looked away, as if to say, "We met before, you cannot trick me." Laughter and joy moved through the group, and Ginger seemed rather pleased with herself. Ginger, at a very young age, was displaying very mature behavior. We all then had a very rich discussion about how old a horse needs to be before they begin this work with teaching humans.

Then we brought our attention to Moon. I began to talk about how to care for an equine herd during programs. While I spoke, I offered Moon a hands-on healing treatment for his now aging and arthritic joints, as he had overextended himself physically the previous day. Moon is a proud horse; he has never been one to allow another to care for him in the presence of a group. He had great pride in the early years of his life, moving cattle across thousands of acres of land. Now, he takes noble pride in his ability to carry a group into the spiritual realms, transporting them beyond the mundane everyday experience here on earth. I was surprised at his willingness to allow me to care for him in front of the group.

As I kneeled at the bottom of Moon's legs and began to work with his joints, he would lift one leg or another to communicate his needs. Slowly his head dropped down, almost touching my back, his eyelids became heavy as he went deeply into a restful state and another realm of consciousness. At this time, I was able to see the beauty of what he was offering the group. Even in his painful moments, his "beingness" was still offering great lessons for those students who were truly present to his "presence." As I spoke, I also watched and felt the energy of each of my students, all having their own experiences within the deep heartfelt energy field created by Moon. Some students dropped deeply into a quiet silence. Others became distracted, unable to be with the potent heart-opening energy offered by Moon. Additionally, the contrast of youthful Ginger with Moon's aging process became a potent mirror. Some knelt to watch intently and locked into the experience of his powerful energy. They were ready and willing to have what he was offering.

Afterward, one student approached me with tears in her eyes. She thanked me for what she experienced as a beautiful demonstration and offering of what give-and-take can be within a relationship. As she hugged me, I then understood why the complexities of relationships were randomly emerging within my mind before the students arrived for this program. I realized how deeply we are all interconnected and that we all wish to experience many of the same things, such as healing and heart connection.

My herd, with Moon leading, was giving me information about the needs of the group and how I could best provide learning and healing for them. If I continue to lead from the insights that they, my herd, offer me, I can teach my students in a way that serves their highest good. Both Moon and Ginger had taught this group the dynamic of relationships. Ginger gave everyone the sweet, thoughtful energy of hello as she moved from each person to the next. Moon brought everyone more in-depth into their heart space and the power of the healing energy found there. He showed and demonstrated that it is just as important to receive love and healing from others as it is to give it.

Now more than ever, I follow the lead of my herd. I watch and listen to the wisdom of the herd when I am with them, and also when I am not physically next to them. They offer me inklings and insights that often my thinking mind does not pick up on. When I follow their lead and allow them to work freely with my students, the most miraculous events transpire.

Moon teaches me that regardless of where his physical body may be, his soul touching mine and our unique dance in the realm that is beyond the ego will never end. By being present with him and receiving all of his wisdom during our earthly existence as he moves into his elder years, I have come to understand the duality and the "oneness" in the physical world and beyond, which is within all relationships.

REFLECTIONS

The dynamics of connection and separation, and give-and-take, are always present in relationships. Relationships are complex, yet very simple when each of the participants actively displays their willingness to give and receive with love, non-judgment, and acceptance. By embracing others for the gifts they provide, we gift ourselves with the expansiveness of their being, and vice versa.

- Where in your life are you in a positive cycle of giving and receiving?
- How can the lesson from Moon heal your life?
- In what way can you give more of yourself without giving away all of yourself?
- Where are you in your stage of life, and what wisdom do you have to offer others?

Moon's Big Heart

I took Moon up for a mellow ride on Rabbit Mountain Open Space nature preserve in Colorado recently. Once up the hill, we meandered through the meadows sprinkled with late summer flowers and cacti. His savvy hooves moved along the rocky field with grace. His glance to the left helped me spot an older-looking coyote that sat very still and quiet on a rock not too far away. He was a larger-sized coyote with a scraggly coat. I imagined he had spent many years on this mountain. The multi-tones of grey in his coat made him blend with the rock. If Moon had not looked at him, I would have missed him completely. The coyote watched us intently, never moving, even sometime later, when we looped back around and crossed along his way again. The coyote sat upright and stared intently at us.

Something is exhilarating and calming about moving through nature with a horse. Every horse offers something different. There is often silence while the sun warms one's face or back. Birds chirping and tall fields of grass swaying in the wind create natural songs. The stress of life fades away. Being with a horse, being carried by a horse, and becoming one with a horse in this way bring life into all of the senses. It is truly a spiritual life-feeding experience.

Moon is my first horse, and riding him that day brought me the deep peace I usually feel with him. However, I was also surprised to feel deep sadness. Moon and I have been together now for some time. I remembered a time when it was just the two of us. I laughed at how much he would challenge me at the start . . . knowing that I had no idea what I was doing. The first day, he put his hind legs deep in a ditch and stood a good long time while I struggled to figure out how to get him out. A nice man in a cowboy hat came to my rescue.

Once we got our relationship going, I had exceptional experiences. I loved our rides on the full moon in the snowy fields. On the extra cold nights, snow-blanketed fields would sparkle like diamonds as Mother Earth made her frost. The warmth of Moon's back spread to the seat of my pants as our bodies melded together in our bareback canter up the big hills. Glass-like snow crystals divided past his chest and fell with magical tinkles of sound. In the warmer seasons we would ride out alone through the canopy of yellow aspens and dark evergreen pines, breathing in the moisture from the land and creeks and connecting to all of nature. After these rides, I would come home and fall into a deep, restful nap, the gift of the ride; his presence decompressed my entire body and being.

I chose to get Corazon when I thought it was time to add another horse to my herd. Corazon was a five-and-a-half-year-old mustang deemed untrainable and unrideable by the Bureau of Land Management. Moon just looked at me with disgust as if to say, "Really, you have got to be kidding me!" He was not happy to have competition for attention, and he and Cor were complete opposites in personality. However, my Moon stood tall and worked his ranching moves as we ponied Corazon over bridges, water, along the trails, and through the fields. I would sit proudly on Moon and have Corazon circling us and doing little tricks. Moon came to terms with Cor, even though he was somewhat of a pest and trying to take over the lead when we ponied him up the snow-covered fields.

Then, I decided to add yet another horse to my herd when Moon's ability to carry a rider was diminishing. I was still keen to ride out in nature, so I found a lovely paint mare of dirty palomino color. She was shiny like a copper penny with a bright blonde mane and tail. She was kind and beautiful. I made the mistake of telling Moon that she would eventually replace him as my riding horse. Stupidly, I introduced them quickly. He ran her down and proceeded to attack her. He was mad as a hornet. I could not blame him. He was my first horse, and he would have been happier without me adding more to the herd because it meant less time for him. When I explained to him that this was his opportunity to have a girlfriend, his attitude changed. Four days later, he was by her side 24–7. Now, when I take her off the ranch, he will cry until we return. However, when she is unloaded from the trailer, he proceeds to pick on her, clearly letting her know he is jealous of our time together.

Moon has touched hundreds of people in my equine facilitated learning sessions. The thing about Moon is that he has given me, and many others, so much of his very big heart. He somehow transitioned from being a working ranch horse on 100,000 acres to working with people in the EFLC work. He has not been the most comfortable horse for many—he speaks and shows the truth, and many are not fully ready for it. He has indeed demonstrated to me the mastery of how to live one's life and how to go through life's transitions while still being true to one's self.

Moon has become the master at working with people on an energetic level, helping to open their hearts to their joys, sorrows, wishes, and desires. He pushes them along like they are the cows in the pastures—the placement of his nose on their body always intentional, always where energy and emotion are locked up. Direct and compassionate, he knows he is the elder, and he knows his job.

As I rode that day with Moon and the old coyote, still sitting and observing us like a sentient horse watching over a herd, I wondered if my sadness was also part of him speaking through me. Today, as I write this, I realize that it was not. This is all mine. The layers of emotion and sadness are my path of letting go, of knowing that he and I will never pony Corazon again, that our days of going up snow-covered hills have come to an end. Though my tears flow as I write, I embrace them, knowing they are helping me to let go when I need to.

Moon and I will still have many years together. Like all relationships, what we do with our years will continue to change. What I do know to be true is that Moon is the horse that has brought me to a deeper place within myself. He is a complex being with his own needs and desires. Moon's soul runs deep like the dark greens, blues, and blacks of the mysterious Atlantic Ocean. I am honored to receive his presence in my life. He has stood by my side and held a space for so much change and growth over the years. In my heart of hearts, I genuinely hope I have done him right. Today, Moon teaches me that things will always change. Just like the seasons of nature, all things have their cycles, and we cannot control them. The only constant we have is how we choose to respond.

As I write this, I sense it may come across as heavy and sounds like a eulogy. To some degree, it is. A part of our life together has run its course, and now I have those moments only in memory. However, Moon is here on earth and on the ranch. Every day he touches a deep part of my spirit and soul. Writing these thoughts makes my heart swell with appreciation. It is the continual exploration and acceptance of the changes in our relationship over time that stretch and open my heart. And later today, when I walk out to hang with the herd, it will be Moon waiting to meet me at the gate, nickering and greeting me as he has done for years.

I hope that you, too, find and have a transformational partnership with a horse in your lifetime. I am blessed with Moon. He will always be my "first love." If you have not had your first horse, your first love, well . . . what are you waiting for?

REFLECTIONS

Whether a relationship is old or new, a healthy one provides opportunities for openness, tolerance, and expansion for each individual. A key to a successful long-term connection is learning to accept the other person's or horse's way of being while maintaining your authentic self. Moon has shown how to stay true to himself, offering a beautiful demonstration of a willingness to adapt to changes. My journey with Moon inspires me to ask and reflect on these questions:

- Am I ready in my life to let go of what was and invite in what might be?
- Am I willing to keep my heart open during transitions?
- Can I trust again after I have been betrayed and disappointed?
- Can I find my place in this world no matter what circumstances are presented?
- Am I willing to risk being wrong to grow and expand?
- Am I willing to let go of who I have been to become more of who I truly am?
- What relationships are transitioning in your life? How will you honor them?

A Dance with Moon—
a Ride Beyond Earth

Moon, my master healer shaman horse, and I danced the other day. It was not an ordinary dance by any means. I am not a circus performer, nor is he. We don't have tricks or practiced moves. Instead, our dance is a moment and a shared, mutually expressed connection.

It was the very last day of a yearlong program. Spring had brought the lush green grass to the land. The fresh green foliage of the trees was bright and joyful against the brilliant powder blue sky. Eight individuals that I had grown very fond of had just facilitated their own highly successful programs with horses at the ranch as part of their graduation process. After passing their final test, our time now was one for enjoyment and celebrating their growth with horses through the last year. The students had little energy, so I volunteered to demonstrate a dancing with horse session. I wanted them to have a visual example and something to ignite their spirit with desire on their return home to their herd.

We headed out to the round, and I felt into my herd to get an intuitive hit on who would be my partner. Moon came forward in my mind's eye, and I went to his paddock and took him to the round pen. The backdrop of the round pen was flush with white and purple blossoms from the spring fruit trees. It was quiet as we entered the round pen. My heart swelled with love for my magnificent horse and for the gratitude I had for the successful year with my eight students. Endings are inevitable and a part of life. It doesn't make them any more comfortable. I released him of the halter in the middle of the round pen, and he was now free to move around as he wished.

I demonstrate these dances with music. Not to recreate synchronistic movement like a performer but instead to create a mood or atmosphere. I always use slow and gentle music with Moon as he is ultrasensitive to both body language and sound. We have done this many other times together. I am still respectful of who he is and how I can best work with him. Our dance is with me on the ground, standing tall and proud to be part of the relationship.

I started the music so Moon could adjust. I had selected beautiful soothing piano music. Gentle notes curved around soft transitions that flowed into the sounds of singing birds and the other herd members releasing their breaths through their lips while watching from the paddock. The students sat quietly and a bit somberly outside the round pen watching Moon and me. I have to be transparent and say that it *always* feels very vulnerable to me when I demonstrate horse dancing. I feel very much on the spot and in a position to be judged. Then I have to remind myself that I have a partner and that the dance is about honoring the partner.

Right before we began, in my mind I asked Moon if he was willing to dance with me; he walked away. In a sudden panic, I thought, *Oh shit. He is not in the mood.* Facing my demons of failure and being judged, I then thought, *Well, I might as well see where we go—it will be perfect no matter what happens.* I allowed my body to absorb the music and become more present in the perfect moment. Then, as I dropped back into my body presence, Moon turned and faced me.

His eyes gazed softly on me. Together we began to move in ease. We circled the round pen side by side. As I walked in tighter circles, he stayed by my shoulder. Then I turned tightly, and he too turned with me, his massive, long, barge-like body turning just as tightly as possible. His hooves were crossing over each other and falling into a pattern similar to mine. As I opened my body and arms back into the entire round pen space, he too opened to it and began a very light small trot around me. We danced like this, moving back and forth. Sometimes we were together, and other times we were not. Sometimes I would walk toward him, and he would softly back up, matching my leg movements. What unfolded and transpired with the beautiful flowing piano music supporting us was ultimately body, mind, and spirit. Moon and I did not do any fancy footwork. I did not try to be clever or look beautiful. Instead, I found my entire presence and heart only with my magnificent friend. All else fell away. He must have felt this because he then returned the heart energy to me. Then, together we went to a place beyond the mundane.

As the music started to wind down further, I could sense the end coming. We came to a still standpoint, and I found myself dropping onto my knee, looking into Moon's deep, almond-shaped, wisdom-filled eyes, his head hanging low in front of me. Time stopped in our mutual lovelock. When I rose, I slowly circled his body and stood next to his hip. I began to stroke his long back, ever so softly, with deep, expansive emotion whelming up inside of me. I could not stop the gentle flow of tears that rolled down my cheeks. Shoulders rounded, my body gone soft, I gained some ground with a few deep breaths, suddenly aware of all of my soon-to-be graduates watching. Moon then turned and circled me and faced all of the students who were just outside the round pen.

With all eyes on him, time stood still, and Moon held sacred space. His eyes and head never moved as he looked at the entire group. Moon went down the row of students, looking at each student intently. It seemed he was highlighting the importance of the energy exchange just demonstrated. He clearly was saying, "This is your work now. Take this possibility out to your people and change the way we, the horses, are seen." There were no dry eyes in the group. There were no words to be shared. Moon, the master of ceremony, gave his blessings and gratitude to the students. Now it was their time to bring the body of work they had learned with me forward and into the world.

Love is not a strong enough word to describe my feelings for Moon. Not one of us had words for that moment in time. That was part of the perfection of it. Words do not convey honor and reverence; they are feelings that flow forth from one's soul. I share this personal story with you because my heart wants you also to have the opportunity to experience something similar. The reverence for all of Mother Nature and her creatures is a gift that is available to us at all times. The only investment we need to make is to see our earth and what she creates not just as vehicles for our accomplishments or endeavors but as gifts from God to bring us into the sweet surrender that is life.

There are gifts everywhere, but often we get too busy with our agendas and we miss the moments. Before you know it, the event is over, and the goodbyes begin. Moon reminded my entire group and me that connection is vital and that endings are inevitable. However, when we are present to where we are in the circle, we take the gift of the experience with us. We have only the moment to seize the day to truly live. Take nothing for granted. Be vulnerable and see where it might take you! More than anything else, the horses continue to show me this.

REFLECTIONS

I invite you to wait no longer to connect or reconnect with your horses and all who are important to you in the most beautiful dance of love. Each day passes quickly, and before you know it, the time will be gone. Have reverence for and honor the sacred bond that exists between beings, and how each of us becomes better for having the connections we do.

- Do you look your animal in the heart and eye?
- Do you embrace their playfulness or their attempts to dance with you in their way?
- Where in your life have you missed celebrating an ending because you were not fully present? What might be possible if you become more conscious of doing so in the future?
- Do you dare to dance with your animal free of judgments?

The Silent One—
a Tribute to Dizzy

Dizzy was a lovely red mare who came to me because she had little hoof wall and was struggling in the rocky pasture where she lived. Beyond that, she had few friends in the herd and was just not that happy. In a life of challenges, Dizzy's pedigree was an exception; she was full of fire when she wanted to be. She had done everything and had given a lot to her humans. A few accidents and some broken bones brought an end to her owner's desire to ride her. Then, she was diagnosed with kissing spines. This condition creates a consistent, low-grade pain along the spine because the bones attached to the vertebrae are too close together and rub or impinge on each other.

When she came to my farm, her body looked heavy and depressed, her eyes were dim, and she carried her head low. Her physical body spoke of pain. Her reluctance to connect with anyone, horse or human, was evident. If one did get close enough to reach out, she would turn and walk away. Distance became the most common observation. My heart told me to give that to her and to let her adjust to her new environment. I had put her with my loving mare, Diva, a mare that welcomed everyone under her wing, sharing food and space, and offering companionship.

For months, the red mare would be as far as she could be out in the five-acre pasture, only coming close at feeding time. Even then, Dizzy would not eat close to my kind mare; she would find a quiet spot where she had plenty of space. Sensing that this mare needed to step up and into the herd when she was ready was easy for me to see and provide for her. However, at times I found her utterly frustrating. Simple tasks to help her, such as putting on her fly mask, could take twenty minutes of relationship-building through negotiating and convincing her that I would not harm her. I was determined not to dominate the mare. I wanted to fully respect her process and boundaries.

When I moved from the larger ranch to my quaint and sweet six-acre farm just a few miles away, things began to shift. The ground on the six acres was softer, and it appeared that her hooves were more comfortable. She and my loving mare became fast friends; however, she still stood away from the others when they would stand as a herd. She was indeed the silent one, the last to come through the gate from the pasture, to get her feed, to be noticed, to have her mask put on or removed, and to receive anything.

One hot day when the herd was in the field, and I was in the paddock next to the canal with a big grandfather cottonwood tree offering shade, I was surprised to turn and see Dizzy standing behind me. My heart swelled with the joy of her sweet and unexpected appearance. She took a step toward me, and I heard: "May I die here?" Surprised not only by the clear communication, but also the content of the question, my hand reached and stroke her dark red neck as I replied: "Yes, of course, you can, and I want you to live here. Your home is here with me forever. You have work to do here if you like." She licked and chewed as we both stood in the truth of the exchange. I was brazen to offer her this promise, as she was not entirely mine. The lovely lady who initially brought her to me still owned her and had no intention of letting her go, as Dizzy was her daughter's first horse. However, Dizzy and I became much closer, and I treated her as if she were my own.

With that heart bond present, my ego changed the message she offered me. I did not want to trust the clarity of my intuition. So, I changed the question to: "Can I live here" because she had approached me in her favorite stall. It was the stall with the big grandfather cottonwood tree that offered shade and peace in the summer, and where during the winter months, the owls would perch at night. From that time on, Dizzy spent most of her nights in that paddock. It was the best paddock, and to honor her request, even though she was a boarded horse, she got it.

The Silent One archetype develops from the need to survive what appears to be a highly incongruent and unsafe world. By being silent and just doing the best they can, without saying much, they do not have to face the ramifications of other's dissatisfactions. It is not worth it to show up. And at the root, worthiness becomes the challenge.

However, the Silent One often brings excellent gifts to us, if we are astute enough to listen and notice. The Silent One has, usually on such subtle levels, an effect on others. The Silent One can often get lost in the herd, creating precisely what they wish: to go unnoticed. Somewhere along their life path, they experienced high levels of rejection, unkindness, inconsideration, neglect, or betrayal. In the worst cases, they may have experienced being physically, emotionally, or spiritually abused, leaving the quiet one distrusting of others and life itself. The coping strategy they employed to survive was to become invisible. The personal needs of the Silent One often go unmet or unfulfilled, and their true self is never honored.

The Silent One often has levels of sensitivity that are beyond the ordinary person's understanding or awareness. Their lack of being seen or getting their needs met is not from their ability to stand tall and make specific requests of others. Their high level of perception and sensitivity around the moods and intentions of others and their environment often puts them in a place of responding to the world as an animal that is preyed upon does, always being aware of others and staying small in order not to be noticed.

It was only a few months after arriving at the smaller farm that Dizzy started to change. She softened. She began to approach me so I could remove or put on her mask. She would stand still and allow me to touch her body. Whatever I did with the rest of my herd, I did with her. I kept telling her how important she was, how safe she was, and that she was part of the herd.

She also stepped into her work in helping humans heal. Many of her first sessions, she would not allow touch, and if she did, it would be a simple stroke or a soft hand on her withers before she would walk away as if that amount of energy was all she could take. But each time, she would try a bit more. She would also stand along the fence line and watch the equine-guided learning sessions. While safely in her paddock, she could see that no harm would come to horses. She could see that only being with humans was required and that however she wanted to respond was entirely acceptable.

It was through this process that Dizzy, the Silent One, felt safe to show up in her authentic self. And each time she did so, more healing would spread through the red mare's heart. Each year, she would offer more and more in the healing sessions with humans. She moved from not allowing touch, to allowing some contact, to in her later years, providing her full, undivided attention to the human she was supporting. In those moments, I would watch her softly place her muzzle on a person's hand, arm, belly, or heart. She would stand and breathe in soft peace.

Tears sprung to my eyes the third summer at the small farm when I watched a student walk to her, connect with her, and share soft hellos and exchanges. Then ever so gently, the student asked Dizzy to walk off and begin a circle. Dizzy, with bright eyes and a relaxed mind and body, followed the student's lead, and the two of them created the most delicate, flowing partnership of weaving energy and beings I had ever witnessed at my farm. Clearly, within that round pen, only the two of them existed. At that moment, I knew that the lovely red mare had gained back part of her authentic self in my programs, and especially with this particular student. Dizzy had come full circle. Her presence was strong and deeply healing for students.

Only nine months later, in the middle of the winter, I noticed I had high anxiety about my herd. Soon, I would start my travels to Arizona for my winter programs. In my mind, I worried that my buckskin, Moon, was getting ready to pass. He and Dizzy were both about to turn twenty-five. Moon is my first horse, and my bond with him is so strong I could not fathom being without him. Locked into this worrying pattern, I could not see beyond it or make sense of the feelings I was having. I had a great deal of anxiety as I packed my bags to head to Arizona to teach.

The day that I left, I was sitting in the waiting area for my gate at the Denver Airport. My worry affected my work, and I found myself sitting in an airport trying to finish an opening speech for the first coaching with horses conference that I had put together. It just so happened that the gate I was sitting at had a wall-sized photograph of a horse with its long shadow cast on the ground. In the picture, the horse was reaching out to touch a person's hand. Loving the synchronicity of my gate being at this mural, I felt an urgency to write. I pulled out my computer, and a poem came flying through my fingertips. I had never desired or attempted to write poetry or prose, but now I felt possessed with urgency as the words came to me.

Simultaneously, I felt emotion erupting from me, and tears begin to run down my cheeks. The moment was potent, powerful, and ripping through my heart. I thought for sure that Moon was the one that inspired the writing that came forth. It was not until after Dizzy's passing four days later that I realized the poem was a gift from her.

She had spoken to me that day in the paddock, asking me to release her. Then, she spoke to me again at the airport. She was telling me that her journey here on the physical earth was ending. She was letting me know of her appreciation of my care for her at my ranch. I had touched her heart. Even as I write this, five years later, I can feel her presence and the power of her healing heart within the center of my being.

In retrospect, on some level, I knew she was getting ready to pass. Before I had left for Arizona, I was out walking around and bumped into her as she was standing alone in one of the paddocks. The rest of the herd was out to pasture. She stepped up to me with intention. At the moment, I noticed how her body seemed heavier, how she appeared tired, and there was new growth of white hair sprinkled in her deep red coat around her eyes and face. I laid my head gently on her white-blazed face, my cheek just below her eye level. Things had certainly changed in our four years together. There we stood, together, with the winter sun warming us, breathing. Tears rolled out of me as I thanked her for all she had given others and me in the programs.

As we stood together, I told her how much I appreciated how she contributed to the healing and expansion of the many people she worked with. I told her how important she was to me and that I also knew she was tired. I affirmed to her that her contribution had not gone unnoticed and that she had healed many hearts. She began to lick and chew. Then I spoke words that I had little thought process around. Instead, they seemed to come from a place deep in my heart and in my intuitive knowing. I affirmed to her that she indeed had suffered hardships in her life. Additionally, I acknowledged to her that I felt many humans might not have understood her. I affirmed to her that when she was ready to leave the earth, that she had my blessings. She could transition when she was ready. The conversation went to a place that I had not anticipated or expected. I stroked her more, scratched her behind her ears, and reflected on our time together.

It took me a few weeks to come to serenity with the divine timing of her passing. Sitting with eight students at a ranch in Arizona after her passing and exploring the archetypes of the Silent One, I discovered that seven of the eight students present carried the "Silent One" archetypal energy. Several of them felt a deep connection with the red mare named Dizzy, one of the students being the individual who had shared the lovely dance in the round pen with her the previous summer. We all went to the river, where we built a cairn for Dizzy. We sat in a circle and shared our appreciation for her presence in our life. Then, we ended with singing and chanting. And as we chanted and tuned together, I could feel her presence still with us, helping us to heal our limitations in speaking up and sharing more of ourselves, to go beyond the Silent One, as she had.

The poem that had moved through me while I was at the airport, *Under the Cottonwood Tree,* had not come to me through my entire herd, nor from Moon, but more specifically through Dizzy. As I sat with this poem after her passing, it all became very apparent; her favorite spot under the cottonwood tree, and the words of owning one's self-worth. Dizzy, the Silent One, was communicating with us the entire time.

The Silent One in any herd, group, tribe, or family communicates differently than what we are accustomed to. Keen observers of their surroundings, you will find a significant presence in the Silent One. What they share can often get brushed aside or lost in the commotion of the activity or other external stimulation. The thoughts or ideas offered by the Silent One can come back around to us, but at those times, we may forget that they were gifted to us by the Silent One, and think they are our own. The Silent One speaks softly, waits to be called on, stands on the edge, and watches life go by because they believe so strongly in their lack of worth.

When I returned from Arizona, I found the remaining four members of my herd heavy and depressed, my young filly insecure, my loving mare with a lost look in her eye; Dizzy had grown to be her best friend in the herd. Cor refused to be touched, and Moon stoically stood off to the side. The next few days, when I would look out to the paddocks from the house, I would see that the herd had left the pasture, and they were standing in the paddock, standing where Dizzy had laid down to pass.

The Silent One may not realize she is a vital part of the community, herd, or family. She may not realize that what she has to offer is of great value and that she needs to bring her energy forward with courage and strength to share it with others. She must learn to find her inner truth and to live by that truth and let go of the thoughts, feelings, and projections she senses from others about her lack of worth.

She may discover her value later in life or after relationships have come to their end because, in those times, others realized what they might have missed. Others might see what was previously unseen, and the real gifts that were offered by the Silent One. When the Silent One is brave, and she trusts deeply, she will resource a sincere, authentic expression within herself. She will see that what she reaps in this process is a great sense of purpose and belonging and knowing exactly who she is while finding the tribe that awaits her gifts.

UNDER THE COTTONWOOD TREE

Come to me beneath the old grandfather cottonwood tree,

where the stream flows gently by and the breeze caresses

the small budding lime foliage of spring.

Here with me, you can rest.

Stand by me; follow the rhythm of my breath,

and soon, your beating heart will slow and soften.

This is not the time to fuss or worry; no time is.

Let the earthy scent of the pine trees fill your lungs

and feel the cool damp air on your skin

as the winter land thaws.

Bring your head to my neck and bury your nostrils in my mane.

Smell me, breathe me, be with me.

We are different you and me,

but if you listen to me deeply, I can show you a way.

A way that is easier, more joyful, and brings deep peace.

Feel my love for you, feel my unspoken connection to you,

there is no need to explain; I know your spirit.

Let the hard edges around your heart heal, expand, and release,

as tears spring to your eyes and you gasp awake,

recognizing your place in the herd.

Yes, you remember—you remember who you are

a beautiful, divine being of God, a being who is created of love

and knows the power of love.

And as we stand here, you and I, there is only love.

And you are whole, and so am I,

nothing needed, nothing desired, we are in harmony.

If you could see what I see,

you would see the golden strands of energy

that extend from your being when love is present.

You do not have to work so hard to be good

you already are.

There is no wrongness of you—

at any time.

The divine love that is you is within you.

Lead with presence; follow with unconditional love,

and you will find that all things will come to you

with more ease, more joy, and more light.

Stand with me under the cottonwood tree

where the roots are strong and the soft light

slips through the flickering leaves above.

Rabbits hop by, the sun moves low,

and the day comes to an end.

You will still find me later, into the night,

still under the cottonwood tree, listening to the howling coyotes,

the far-away barking dog and the mating owls hooting

for each other.

And soon the big yellow moon, the essence of my very soul,

will rise and shine in all her glory,

casting shadows and light on the land

and in your consciousness.

My four hooves were firmly planted on this earth,

resisting nothing and embracing all.

The orchestra of life within me, I am in union,

I am one with all.

And here I stand now, in spirit.

I wait, for you, with my heart open, under the cottonwood tree.

REFLECTIONS

Still waters run deep, and so does the Silent One. But when gentle effort and compassion are provided, you can help those wise souls encounter the world in a safe, respectful way. The Silent One observes from a place of safety, seeing a wide perspective of deep layers. When they reveal themselves, the depths of their knowledge and wisdom are often surprising. Whether a horse or human, when you encounter them, let them show themselves and their wisdom in their own way, and you will know the true depths of their being.

- Are you a Silent One?
- Where in your herd or community do you feel you can best serve?
- Where in your life could you reveal more of yourself in a safe way?
- How can you support the Silent Ones in your life?

Keeping Your Grieving Herd Healthy

Afficient my beautiful red mare Dizzy died, I came home to a grieving herd. I had been teaching in Arizona when she passed away. Being away at the time was hard for me, and I was anxious to return home to be with the rest of the herd.

When I arrived home, the remaining members of the herd looked worn out. The skin around their eyes was full of wrinkles and creases, giving them a heavy, sad look. Their bodies appeared to be tired and thick as they sluggishly moved around, dragging their rear legs along behind them. Of the four, only one was willing to allow me to approach and offer physical touch. My mustang quickly walked away when I reached out. Diva, my mare who was closest to Dizzy, moved away from me, with a tired, empty look in her eyes. Moon stood stoic and cool, off to the side, not even bothering to look my way. The youngest of the herd was the only one who approached. Ginger, the two-year-old filly, walked directly to me and pressed her entire head into my armpit, burying her face and quietly standing as I stroked her mane and shoulder and comforted her.

I had not known what to expect because, in fifteen years of having horses, this was my first time losing a herd member. While I respected the distance that the other three horses showed they needed, I found the spot on the ground where the red mare had laid down when she passed.

The morning Dizzy passed, I instructed my pet-sitter to open up all of the gates to allow the herd to move freely between the pasture and the paddock where she lay. My pet-sitter informed me that the horses exhibited a confusing process that morning. They all ran out to the muddy, snow-patched pasture, only to return to the paddock minutes later, looking at Dizzy's body, confused about why she was not getting up. They then went back to the pasture.

Slowly over the next hour, each one came in to check on Dizzy. They stood near her, then lowered their heads and sniffed, trying to comprehend what was happening. Slowly, each one digested that Dizzy's body lay quietly on the ground, but her spirit was no longer there. Some of them circled her, sniffing at different places. Moon stood above her with his long neck stretched over her heart as if he was watching over and protecting a young sleeping foal. Each horse had its own way of reconciling the lack of movement from the red mare's body. Eventually, they all remained in the pasture. By afternoon, the men came to remove Dizzy's body. This gave plenty of time for Dizzy's owner, and my herd, to at least begin to digest the shock of her passing.

Later, it was determined that Dizzy had passed gently, probably from a heart attack, with no apparent pain or struggle because the snow angel she left was one of grace, not struggle or rolling that would happen with colic. I could still see her imprint on the cold, packed snow spot under the evergreen tree when I returned from my trip. It was the coldest spot in the entire area. So, there I kneeled and said goodbye to the horse that had already left days before.

I knew the herd members needed support, but not through touch or physical comfort, at least not yet. They would let me know when they were ready to connect physically with me. It was not uncommon for them to be cool and distant from me when I had been traveling. However, given we had lost a herd member, my desire for connection and touch was strong. I continued to respect the body language they offered that clearly indicated they needed distance—all but the baby of the herd, Ginger, of course. Then, I remembered that I was gifted a box of flower essences. I have used flower essences several times for many different reasons and had witnessed significant positive shifts in the attitude, mood, and emotional status of the horses for various reasons, from resistance in training to defensiveness in treating their physical bodies, and depression or despondence.

When horses are living in the wild, they forage for the needed minerals and plants to aid their body back to good health. In the summer, they are at high elevations enjoying the fresh blooms of mountain purple asters, lupines, Indian paintbrush, and many other wildflowers. As late fall comes, they move to lower elevations where they can access thistle, blanket flower, and sage. Throughout the year, they can find the bark of pine, alder, birch, and aspen. In desert environments, they find cactus, sage, or mesquite. As they roam, they learn to digest what is best for their body and helps them to maintain good health both physically and energetically. In the wild, horses are not grazers; they are foragers. They can require up to twenty-five or more different types of plants in a day. These plants adjust their hormones, provide vitamins, support their nervous system, and detox their system when needed.

Horses today, however, generally live on pasture that consists primarily of grass, or worse, a dry paddock. What the natural world offers is severely limited in these conditions, so horses often receive the minerals and nutrients they need through supplements. However, these supplements do not replace what may be found in a live and vibrant wild environment. A wild environment offers what can be consumed through foraging. However, the wild environment where the horse is foraging also provides the opportunity for the integration of energy that is given off by the plants, trees, grasses, shrubs, and land. Mountain streams, brooks, and lakes give off large amounts of negative ions that help to balance the body and reduce stress. Compare the energy or vibration of New York City to that of a high mountain valley. They are vastly different. Each environment offers a unique "energetic offering."

Flower essences are a way to bring the "energetic offering" of a plant or tree to a human or horse; it is not a supplement that we digest through eating, such as plants and vitamins. Instead, flower essences provide the vibration or energetic offering of the plant to help balance our energetic and emotional system. Not harmful in any way, it is the best first aid kit you can use to support your working herd on a mental, emotional, and spiritual level. They come in a liquid that contains potentized plant "essence," which conveys a distinct imprint or pattern of a specific flower or plant. Each flower or plant can support the etheric level of any living being, joining the spiritual, mental, emotional, and physical aspects of our being for healing. I chose to muscle test each of the herd members to see what flower essences would support them in this process. Ironically, each of the four members of the herd muscle-tested strong to receive one or two of three different essences: red chestnut, water violet, and walnut.

Bach® Original Flower Remedies offers a list of questions for each flower that highlight the challenges one might be facing. These are great for identification—but then what? I pulled out my small deck of cards called Affirm a Flower (a publication of the Flower Essence Society.org) that offer positive, affirming sentences to help with the transition into the next phase of consciousness for each flower essence. I focus on the positive affirming statements because those statements have a higher vibrational frequency. Here are the three essences with the meaning provided by Bach® followed by the positive statements provided by the Affirm a Flower cards:

Red Chestnut

Bach®: Shows up when one is concerned about a loved one, or distressed or disturbed by other's situations, or worry that harm will/has come to those you love.

Affirm a Flower: I remain calm despite my concern for others. My soul finds its spacious center. I send blessings to others.

Water Violet

Bach®: Shows up when one appears to be aloof and overly proud, withdrawn, or alone, when faced with external stress, or when one bears grief and sorrow without talking to others.

Affirm a Flower: My soul knows purity and containment. From this holy sanctuary, I seek connection. My gift is my presence in this world.

Walnut

Bach®: A change in life (or relationships), draining situations, a break from strong attachments.

Affirm a Flower: I relinquish the past and step toward my future. I welcome new possibilities. My Star of Destiny shines brightly on Earth.

I combined the three essences in one tincture bottle with some filtered water and took it out to the herd. Ginger approached first, so I took a dropper of the fluid and placed it in my palm. She proceeded to lick and lick and lick the palm of my hand. Then one by one, each member of the herd approached me. I put more liquid in the palm of my hand, and they did the same thing. Every time I have offered flower essences, I do it in this way, so the horse has a choice to receive it or not. Each time the horse has taken it. Witnessing how many times a horse will lick my palm is extraordinary. Most of the time, they will stand and lick many times. I offered the tincture twice a day for three days. Soon they were eagerly approaching me, one pushing the other away to be next to lick my hand.

Each day, the herd would also come in from the pasture during the afternoon and stand as a collective on the spot that Dizzy passed. They would stand there silently and still for hours. It was their spot to grieve, to process, to say goodbye, and to give respect to the lost member of their herd. The herd began to look a little different each day. A bit more light came back into their eyes. They also then started to reconnect with me and ask for a stroke on their neck, a scratch on their chest. Then they would lick and chew, stretch their heads to the sky, and return to lick and chew some more. On day four, no one wanted to lick the liquid of the flower essence from my palm. They also did not come in from the pasture to stand on Dizzy's spot. Instead, I found them on the far side of the paddock, under a big cottonwood tree.

For me, grieving Dizzy has been a continual process with many nuances. Regrets of missed opportunity (could I have done better by her?), missing her and sensing her at feeding time (turning and expecting to see her—only to find she is not there), anger for her leaving (after she had grown so magnificently into her work with humans), anger at self for not hearing her messages to me (instead of assuming they were from Moon), and the broken heart of not being there when she passed. Like my horses, I must give myself time to process. I must also support my being in the ways that work for me (reflection, sharing through conversation, ritual, flower essences), and I must remain calm despite my concern for others. My soul finds its spacious center. I send blessings to others.

My herd and I send you blessings. We encourage you to find ways to take good care of yourself during times of deep change and of releasing and accepting. We trust and hope that you know and that you always come back to the thoughts that spread love, healing, and positivity into your spirit. I relinquish the past and step toward my future. I welcome new possibilities. My Star of Destiny shines brightly on Earth.

REFLECTIONS

Trying to bypass the process of grief and the journey that this emotion (and all emotion) takes us on is unhealthy. When we learn to allow the nuances of emotion and energy to move through us, we are truly experiencing a richness of life. We all experience grief in our lives at some point, whether it's death, the end of a relationship, or some other ending. We all experience the grieving process differently and at different rates of healing. The important part of the process is to feel the emotions and continue to move through them using the tools that work best for you.

- How do you process loss?
- What tools do you use to help you move through the emotions that loss can bring to the surface?
- How can you let others know what you need when you experience loss?
- How can you help others through loss in the most loving and supportive way?

PART III
Horse as Teacher and Healer

Being versus Doing with Horses

During an equine facilitated and coaching workshop in Arizona, I had the privilege of working with a beautiful Percheron. Kairos is the most massive horse I have ever seen, well over seventeen hands. His physical body is grounding and calming. His gentle nature makes time stand still. His slow-moving, solid black muscular mass calls you to him and pulls you back in time.

Originating in Le Perche near Normandy in France, Percherons were used as war horses, carrying knights into battle. They are usually grey or black. The breed characteristics are light, sure-footed, and spirited. As agricultural pursuits began to take precedence over fighting, the Percheron was bred more for size, weight, and strength. The direct lines of breeding are unknown, but as times changed and machinery replaced horses, the breed began to fade. In 1954, only eighty-five head of Percheron were recorded alive. They are truly gentle giants, and their pleasing personalities make them very willing to work with humans. Since then, they have made a strong comeback and have gained in popularity.

At the workshop, Kairos offered participants an equine learning experience in "being" versus "doing." Several people reported that they felt a deep sense of communion and connection to something beyond words by merely being near him. They said they felt more present and connected to the earth, as if time itself was slowing down. Kairos's complete focus and gentle gestures moved people to the depths of their consciousness.

While facilitating one woman, Darlene, in a reflective round pen session, I shared the same experience of moving deeper into a timeless place and sense of consciousness. At the time, I was facilitating equine learning sessions in the round pen. During these sessions, the client stands outside and prepares to enter the pen with the horse. I lead them through several questions that help them become more aware of their bodies and the desires held in their hearts. Darlene's hope with Kairos was to experience a deep sense of peace and for time to stand still. Even as she said the words out loud, Kairos, who was at the opposite side of the round pen, turned his massive body and moved toward us, each hoof landing heavily on the sand as he came. My client was already feeling profound healing energy emerging from inside of herself as she connected to this gentle giant's magnitude.

Typically, a horse's heart can be seven to ten times larger than a human heart. In this case, I am sure that Kairos's heart was well beyond ten times more massive. He was the biggest horse I had ever worked with in this reflective styled session. Yet, there was nothing to fear about him. He moved slowly, his demeanor was calm, and nothing seemed to bother him.

My client entered and stood in the center of the round pen. As she did so, Kairos turned to watch her. The three of us made a triangle formation. I noticed that my breath began to slow down. It was also deepening from coming into my lungs and into my stomach and entire body. It has been a while since I had felt my breath to this degree. Kairos looked at me, and then as if in recognition, turned his attention to Darlene. Darlene looked petite in comparison to Kairos. Her long, straight blonde hair hung down her spine and shimmered in the bright light. Kairos, on the other hand, was a pure, deep, and endless black. His dark eyes intently gazed upon her, and he began to lick and chew. I could also see calmness in Darlene's body and eyes as their sense of each other deepened.

I felt a direct, clear, pure stream of soft energy moving from Kairos to the center of Darlene's heart. I immediately felt my heart expand with warm fluidity and stretch beyond where it had ever previously experienced. Soft tears came to my eyes. The tears were not of sadness or fear, but of recognition. At that suspended moment in time, an unspoken connection and knowledge passed from Kairos to Darlene and then to me. This unspoken sense of knowing felt like a complete book of knowledge, a sense of expansion and depth much more significant than anything I have ever experienced with any other horse. It was as if the wisdom of all of the ages was shared with us. Time stood still. No questions to ask and no answers to explore, an empty moment simultaneously containing all the wisdom of the universe. The sense of infinity was palpable, and time became irrelevant. The three of us stood, unmoving in this energy for several moments as a flock of birds sang in the nearby trees and the horses close by laid down to nap. Everyone was experiencing something profoundly deep.

If you meditate or commune with nature, you may have a sense of what I'm describing. You have experienced those delicious moments beyond words, the moments when you feel you are one with everything while the wisdom of the ages sinks into your cells. In Ancient Greek, *kairos* means the right, critical, or opportune moment. Biblically, the word kairos is connected to a moment of grace and it can signify a time of change or conversion. It can also mean to create a perfect moment to deliver a particular message. As a gentle giant, the power of Kairos took us to a significant moment, effortlessly, as if it is where he resides the majority of the time.

I seek those moments of experience, bottomless, vast in circumference, and endless in time. With his sensual, prehistoric, and calming energy, Kairos invited all of us to venture into that infinite state of connection with all. The moment was one of being, not doing. Even as the coach for my client, I benefited from the gift shared by Kairos. These moments of surprise of depth and beauty are why I partner with horses in this way.

Finding the right words to express the unique way horses help humans grow their awareness has been thought-provoking. I have chosen to use the Equine Facilitated Learning and Coaching (EFLC) program because it includes the horse and the human as partners in providing personal and professional growth experiences for individuals and groups.

In finding the right terms, I reflected on the meaning of each word:

Equine: A horse.

Facilitate: To make easier or less difficult, help forward (an action, a process, understanding, etc.), and assist the progress or growth of (a person).

Learning: The acquisition and development of memories and behaviors, including skills, knowledge, understanding, values, and wisdom. It is the product of experience and the goal of education. Learning ranges from simple forms of learning such as habituation and classical conditioning seen in many animal species to more complex play activities seen only in relatively intelligent animals.

Coaching: A form of communication that provides exploration, insight, clarity, and direction for a person or group of people to enhance and succeed in personal or professional advancement and achievement.

I concluded that a horse in its natural state of being is a mirror, healer, and teacher for humans. By interacting with horses in a setting that encourages awareness of body, mind, and spirit, humans learn. Clients gain new skills, knowledge, behaviors, and understanding about themselves and others. The coach (human), through a coaching conversation (after the session), helps the client apply the learning into other areas of their life.

Equine Facilitated Learning and Coaching (EFLC) is based on the philosophy that through creating relationships with horses, a person may explore and learn new ways of understanding how they interact with the world around them. Horses are nonjudgmental beings that facilitate learning positively and immediately. Learning a life lesson from a half-ton horse is often easier than through a friend, supervisor, or business partner. Horses do not have preestablished judgments or defensive posturing that often blocks learning experiences with our human counterparts.

During sessions with horses, the horse's nature brings to the surface behaviors, habits, and skill levels of the client. When a person reaches new self-awareness levels, higher levels of trust, intimacy, and respect are achieved with a horse. The learning happens as a visceral experience and lodges deeply into the memory cells of the body. Through understanding the horse and the horse's nature, and learning in the moment how to best communicate with horses, the human's growth is exponential. Only through significant levels of understanding and mutual acceptance and awareness can more intelligent communication levels emerge.

The programs I facilitate honor the horse for the teachings they provide and offer additional support through a coaching conversation. An experienced, trained coach has the conversation and communication skills and tools to help the client fully understand their equine experience and how to apply that experience into their everyday life. As a trained and seasoned business and life coach, I am dedicated to providing a process for the impact of working with a horse to make substantial changes in a person's life and relationships and to succeed in living with purpose in the world.

I have experienced many sessions similar to the one with Kairos. I believe a significant part of the EFLC experience is in "being" in a place of grace and significant timelessness with the horse. However, many equine experiential learning programs focus on "doing" something with a horse to have an equine experience. I recently offered a presentation in Boulder, Colorado. One participant criticized the equine-based demos I facilitated. She claimed the sessions were not experiential enough. This participant needed to touch or interact with the horse to have an experience. I see value in physically interacting with horses. I also know the importance of connecting through non-doing activities, thus encouraging people to experience through the energy of their hearts versus their heads.

What quantifies an experience? Do we have to touch or be physical to have a sense of experience? Must we play games, have goals, agendas, and protocols, or even ride to feel we have fully experienced the horse? An experience is defined by recognizing and gaining knowledge or comprehension through observation or interaction. Achieving an experience can happen by simply "being" versus "doing."

I believe we can reach more profound levels of experience by "being." Our doing nature puts us into our heads, fills us with itineraries, and removes us from feeling with our hearts. When we choose to "be," we also breathe, feel, observe, and accept the moment and connect with another. There is no time for judgment or analysis. That is the beauty of being with horses.

REFLECTIONS

Think of a time that the soul of another's presence has touched you. I imagine that the person or animal was very grounded and aware of you, yet not asking for you to be any different than you are at that moment. Their presence alone compelled you into a deeper understanding of yourself and your heart energy without words exchanged. Your heart may have expanded or dramatically healed through the event.

- When is the last time you sat in the company of another being (horse or human) without agenda?
- What did you experience when you shared this moment in time?
- Are you more focused on making the experience happen, or are you willing to let the experience unfold naturally?
- Must you always be doing, or are you willing to only bond through being?

The Horse's Way:
Heartfelt Appreciation with Viejo

Viejo had lived wild on the vast drylands of Arizona for several years before he was unfortunately captured and brought into the human world. Instead of moving about the earth as he pleased in search of water and food, he became part of a herd in Southern Arizona. He was with many others like him, living in a barren, dry, dusty corral surrounded by mesquite brush. He had his friends and also the horses he preferred to avoid.

Each day, the herd watched the rental cars drive by with city slickers behind the wheel and well-manicured passengers looking at their cell phones. In the mornings, the horses lined up, got tacked up in leather saddles, and waited for guests to saunter down to the livery. There, one by one, the humans mounted a trusted steed. Once all the guests were secured and fully prepared, the group slowly moved out for the first ride of the day. The guides, always with a classic cowboy hat on his or her head, led, and the horses followed head to tail out to the high desert where old mining shafts and remains abounded.

Viejo is a dude ranch horse. Luckily for him, he landed at a resort that loves their horses and treats them well. But when I arrived, he looked a bit scruffy. It was midwinter, and his coat was filled in. I could see the sweat marks from where the saddle had been on his back. His long black socks, black mane and tail, and caramel coat were the colors of a buckskin horse. A typical quarter horse tends to be medium in build and more massive in front around their chest and shoulders. As a mustang, Viejo had powerful large hooves, and his body was slender and taller than his quarter-horse friends. His legs were long and narrow. There was nothing grandiose about his appearance. He was an unassuming ranch horse. His name, Viejo, means old man in Spanish.

I decided to have him in my program because there seemed to be something unusual about him. Although he seemed agreeable, I also sensed another layer of his personality that felt hidden, saved for only those who he deemed ready or deserving of experiencing. Beyond that, I have an affinity for mustangs. I sense that many of them have much more to say than the general public is ready to listen to or can hear. It was obvious to me that Viejo would offer a golden nugget of learning for someone.

In equine learning sessions, many horses demonstrate fascinating and engaging behaviors. I have seen horses lie down, protectively walk around the client, bow, pick up the carrot stick or lunging whip and hand it to the client, point their nose at certain areas of the client's body, and completely back up all the way across a penned area so that their butt is next to the client. All of these gestures are communications and can mean different things depending on the setting and what the client is processing. Once the horse figures out that nothing is expected of him in the typical way, he can step into being a teacher. The horse often becomes a mirror of the emotional and mental content of the client's internal landscape.

Some horses will stand completely still to offer support to the client, sometimes even dropping into an altered breathing cycle (that I interpret as shamanic breath). The quality of breath enhances stillness in the present moment and often drops the client deep into their heart space. Other clients experience a sense of going "between the worlds" or momentarily experiencing a shift in their consciousness. That is the beauty of working with horses. As highly in-tune animals, they offer forms of communication that are beyond what one might expect.

For many years, horses have been seen as a means to an end. They are used to get a job done. They carry humans on their backs in war, leisure events, competition, working a ranch, or parades. They have pulled wagons, plowed fields, and hauled timber from our forests. Now, many of them are employed to be a teacher for humans. These horses help humans understand what they are communicating at unconscious levels, among many other things.

Viejo proved himself to be a master teacher. He did what I have seen and experienced many intelligent mustangs do while interacting with humans—gave direct and honest feedback to the human about her state of emotions and internal thought processes. This particular week of study, I was teaching my students the key elements for coaching and supporting others in equine learning sessions. We had shifted out of quiet, contemplative activities into active exercises where the client, while interacting with a horse, could explore leadership skills, set boundaries, and learn how to modulate their energy.

For this activity, we were sitting at a round-shaped pen, a classical area where most trainers work or train a horse and where many riders will warm up their horse. The person then instructs the horse to move forward at different levels of gaits, such as a walk, trot, or a canter, to come forward or stop entirely. The horse is at complete liberty with no halter on its head or lead line attached to them. The client prepares for this experience by using the lunging whip or carrot stick outside of the pen. They practice the proper and respectful way to communicate to the horse and how to create different levels of energy expression through the tool and their body somatic. The client learns to stay safe and create a boundary with a horse. They become comfortable using the carrot stick, which gives them more ease once they enter the round pen.

The session starts as the coach and client stand outside of the round pen while the horse is free to roam about inside as it wishes. The coach then leads the client through a process to create congruence in their body and mind. Horses respond well to people who are congruent and do not trust those who are not. When a person is congruent in what they are thinking, their mind and feeling in their body are the same. An incongruent person would be a person who says they feel confident and ready to work with a horse, but inside they are experiencing fearful thoughts such as *what is this horse going to do? What if I fail? I am going to be judged by others. I had better get this right. I can't be wrong. I am scared but don't want to admit it.* Their body, responding to these deep-seated and often ignored thoughts, prepares to fight, freeze, or flight. The horse, being a very in-tune being, will begin to sense that energy. Highly tuned horses will smell the change in chemistry of a human being's adrenaline when it becomes activated. The horse's internal strength determines if the horse decides to take the lead or get reactive to the human who has unconsciously projected fear into the round pen area.

There is a vast difference between a quiet, reflective, and contemplative session and a session that is about getting into action. These inspiring sessions are active and engaging. However, sometimes the horse guides us in a different direction. It is always lovely and encouraging when a client enters in with the horse, makes a connection, and then proceeds to have success with their horse. An instant bond and understanding of communication is not the usual experience.

Many horses are trained in the round pen to such an extent that they will simply do whatever the human asks. Their own instinctual responses are conditioned out of them and they learn to only comply to their handler's wishes. I teach the horse that their mind needs to be engaged. The horse learns to allow their natural way of being a horse to come forward by responding to the energy offered, just as they would in a herd. One of the reasons I love working at this dude ranch is that they seldom put their horses in a round pen. In fact, they build a round pen for me when I bring my group. So, I know which horses have had some experience, and I also know that they don't do this a lot, so their feedback is going to be direct, unconditioned, and immediate.

It is not uncommon that when the scene shifts from an intention focused on being present to then creating action with the horse, many things can transpire that indicate a deep resonance and understanding between horse and human. Other times, the opposite is true, and the horse will show the human where they may have lost connection within themselves and the present moment.

I worked with my client outside of the round pen. Viejo was inside, calming, walking around. The sun was warm, and there was a slight breeze. The big red barn sat behind us, and mesquite brush surrounded the arena. The desert scents were strong but fresh and uplifting because it had rained the night before.

I coached my client, Janice, to become more present and congruent at the moment. Janice was a very gentle and kindhearted individual. She was thoughtful, and her energy was calm. Janice seldom got overly excited or changed her demeanor much at all. She declared that she wanted Viejo to move forward in a walk, trot, and canter. Janice said if she could do this with the horse, then she could move her business in the direction she wanted without hesitation, creating positive success.

Once inside, Janice approached Viejo and stroked him a few times on his neck. He stood quietly and seemed to be enjoying the touch. Then Janice moved to the center of the round pen. She asked Viejo to begin to circle the round pen. This student gently lifted the carrot stick as part of her process of questioning. Viejo willingly moved off in a gentle trot around the edge of the round pen with lightness. Immediately, I noticed that Janice did not "stop asking" with her tool. The respectful communication would allow the tip of the carrot stick to come down to the sand, taking pressure off the horse and acknowledging the conversation that was successful with the horse. Instead, Janice lifted the stick not once, but twice, continuing to ask. The mood and energy I saw in Janice were different than what she usually demonstrated. I sensed that this was an unconscious action from my client. I also watched Viejo interpret the gesture of keeping the stick high to communicate, "You are still not doing it."

Viejo is an older horse in his late teens. He has seen a lot in the wild, and then he spent many years as a working horse on a cattle ranch. His knowledge and wisdom are in-depth, and his ability to read humans is profound. He was well trained, so he knew how to respond to the tools we were using and quickly understood his role as a teacher. At that moment, he began to teach Janice.

Viejo stopped abruptly and stood still. The student digressed into a more assertive behavior by shaking the stick and trying to motivate him along. I sensed that Janice was becoming a bit anxious that he had stopped, and she was surprised and unsure of what to do. Her response was to keep asking by waving the stick. Viejo kept standing, parallel to the panels, and looking ahead, not giving her any attention at all.

I immediately started to work with Janice, asking her questions such as, "What just happened between the two of you? What do you suppose he is telling you? Are you aware of how you were holding the carrot stick? Are you aware of what you were doing with the carrot stick?" Janice stood, and I noticed her shallow breathing. Her eyes were big with questions and a touch of nervousness. She did not want to be wrong.

The depth of coaching began at this moment. Once I offered and shared with Janice what I saw, she quickly understood that she had continued to ask for something from Viejo, even though the horse had already given way to her request and instruction. She confessed that she behaves the same at home, too, often getting the same results with her horses. Some might call this nagging. However, in this situation, we reframed it to *not seeing the give.*

I coached Janice to feel the energy of the interaction in her body. She felt a lot of energy stirring around in her lower belly and was embarrassed that she did not see his communication. She could feel how she came out of her awareness of herself and his needs during this interaction with Viejo. Then, the coaching became even more profound. Janice explored the need to do and achieve, which caused pushing or constant pressure on Viejo, in contrast to that of "being."

We also explored what the horse might need, at this moment in their relationship, to feel partnership and respect. Janice wanted to build a more reliable connection through her heart with Viejo, so she centered back into her heart space and started to articulate out loud what she appreciated about him. Janice shared with Viejo that she saw and recognized his spirit and essence (not focusing on what he could do for her).

As she did so, I could sense the emotion of gratitude rise within her as her body softened. At the same time, Viejo ever so softly lifted one hoof and moved it slightly toward her.

At first, she did not see the gesture from Viejo. I gently pointed it out to her. Janice then continued to share her gratitude for Viejo from her heart. As she did so, Viejo's body and eyes softened even more, and he lifted his hoof again to inch a bit closer. Janice looked at me with her eyes wide open, understanding the profoundness and subtlety of the experience. She understood the significance of sharing genuine affirming thoughts directly from her heart to his heart as part of laying the foundation of communication and connection with Viejo. It created a positive field of heart coherence with Viejo. Janice realized how important having a connection and relationship with another is in partnership. To simply ask, and continue to ask, and expect to get it was insensitive. She came to understand that how the other is feeling about the request and giving positive feelings toward another could keep a loving flow of creative energy between them. To do this, she would have to pay attention to the other's feelings, communications, and personal requirements.

One more time, she centered in her heart and said out loud what she appreciated about Viejo and the wisdom of all horses. Viejo responded by stepping forward and placing his nose on Janice's heart. There they took several moments together.

Everyone sitting in the circle also felt this profound moment that Viejo, as a teacher and spiritual guide, had offered, not only to the individual but to all of us. The sensitivity of his offering and the stoic way in which he taught was nothing short of magnificent. Many of us experienced tears of recognition, of the way things should be, that Viejo guided us to see. Even as I write this, I return to that moment with him and my client, and my heart swells with gratitude for all horses and their beauty and kindness in teaching humans "the horse's way."

THE HORSE'S WAY: HEARTFELT APPRECIATION WITH VIEJO

Horses are gentle, loving teachers, and the more I work with them, the more I see how they appreciate the important work they are allowed to do. Each horse is different, just as each client is, and each experience is new and unique. Allowing the horse to become the teacher while coaching humans to receive their wisdom is a gratifying and electrifying experience.

- Are you willing to allow your horse to become your teacher?
- What could you learn from being with a horse in this way?
- What do you appreciate about what your horse teaches you?
- What can you do to build a relationship of respect and trust with your horse to open the channels of teaching and learning?

I Am Unshakable

Stacy was around thirty years old. Her bright carrot hair was curly, stacked on her head in a very playful manner. She had a lot of light energy and a very joyful spirit, yet she was also suffering from angst and continual worry. She feared almost everything she did when she interacted with others. She worried that they would reject her; that she would step on toes; that she would do the wrong thing. She was mostly concerned that if she allowed herself to relax and be who she was, people would leave her. She had learned somewhere along her life path that her energy was too big; that she was too much. If she let herself shine and be alive in the moment, people would turn away.

Stacy was more invested in keeping people close to her than allowing herself to be who she truly was. This is not uncommon. I see this often with people who come to work with me. It's something the horses help people work through in our sessions. We all have pieces of ourselves that we ignore or push away. We modify ourselves to belong to our family of origin, the family we have created, or the community. We have a very high need to belong, just like horses do. No man is an island, and every human needs other human beings in their life to survive and thrive. We all need that sense of connection and protection we get by being with others. It's an essential, fundamental requirement for every human being—or horse—to have a vibrant and thriving existence and life. We all need to belong.

Stacy continually showed signs of nervousness and discomfort during the workshop portion of the program. I had a sense that she would have a significant discovery with one of my horses. At first, I was a bit nervous when she picked my big white mare, Esperanza, to be her teacher. Esperanza is the newest horse in my herd. She's half Arab and half Friesian. For the most part, she is a very friendly horse. She has big, brilliant, and beautiful energy, just like Stacy. However, Esperanza has no problem expressing her energy and shows up exactly who she is in the moment. I've never seen Esperanza shrink at any time for any reason. Esperanza is also highly intelligent. She's a lead mare and demonstrates her bold, large energy continually, never being apologetic for who she is.

Esperanza has also often demonstrated a degree of impatience or a way of letting clients know when they are incongruent. Incongruency is when someone keeps their feelings inside and presents a different energy or mood to the horse than what they are truly feeling. People become incongruent when they can't handle or be with the energy that is arising in their body. If it's too uncomfortable to feel their fear, vulnerability, anxiety, hurt, or frustration, they will stuff those feelings away, dissociate from them, or run away from them.

Stacy would not present incongruencies; instead, she would have a bit of shake in her body, and you could quickly tell when she was uncomfortable or upset. I considered this when Stacy requested to work with Esperanza. In the past, when I've had clients work with Esperanza who are incongruent, Esperanza gets impatient. The way she expresses her impatience is to get a little bit "mouthy" and sometimes try to nip somebody. You can imagine this is problematic for the person providing professional sessions with horses. I certainly don't want someone walking away having been bitten. In the fifteen years and hundreds of people I have served, only once has a client been nipped by a horse, and it was because she was highly incongruent.

I considered Esperanza's tendencies to be impatient with people's incongruencies and Stacy's high levels of anxiety and fear before I decided to allow them to work together. I slept on it overnight, and the next day it was clear to me that things would go as they needed to go. I could help Stacy create good boundaries with Esperanza so she wouldn't get bitten. I'd also developed a trust with Esperanza because I'd worked with her for a year and a half. I knew her personality much more than when she first arrived. She was stepping into being a much higher level teacher than when she first arrived. She understood the parameters much better, and she was much more willing, having come into a much greater level of belonging in her herd. She felt more secure in her interactions with others.

As Stacy and I stood outside the round pen, I led her through some body processes that helped her become fully present so that she could be full of all of the emotion and energy that was arising in her body. Every time Stacy brought her attention inside her body and named where she was sensing energy and what it felt like, Esperanza would walk directly to her, lower her head, and stare at her. As Stacy began to have a dialogue around what was happening and mentalize her feelings, Esperanza would walk away, go to the other side of the pen, play with the canvas we'd set up, nip at the rabbits running by, and show signs of being distracted or uninterested.

I led Stacy through this process for a few minutes and eventually asked Stacy to name her greatest desire for what she wanted to experience with Esperanza. She said she wanted Esperanza to connect with her, to come over and be with her physically and stay with her. I asked Stacy what it would give her if Esperanza did this, what would be the purpose of that action? Stacy replied that it would tell her that she could be who she is and still be loved and feel connected to others. She would know then that people wouldn't leave her if she allowed herself to be fully authentic. Esperanza turned, walked over, and stared at Stacy. I knew at that moment the session would be perfect, and that Stacy would get whatever it was that she needed to step into more ownership of her beautiful big energy and personality.

To prepare my client correctly, I let Stacy know that Esperanza could push into people's boundaries, that sometimes she didn't recognize people's space. I also let her know that she could use her mouth, not to make her fearful, but to have awareness. I also suggested that I move the carrot stick closer to the gate so that if she needed to set a boundary with Esperanza she could easily pick it up and do so. I also let her know that Esperanza is highly sensitive, and if she decided to use the stick (we'd already practiced with it, so she knew how to use it), she would need to use it in a very sensitive manner. If she swung it around, Esperanza would become very high-headed, high-strung, and run around the round pen.

I wanted to prepare my client but not bring fear into her. Stacy received the information in a very balanced, grounded way. She'd worked with horses before in this way, so the work was not completely new to her. Stacy continued to be in her body and feel her discomfort. And then, of course, she'd go into her head and try to understand it or intellectualize it. So she had a very distinct pattern of going back and forth.

Once in the round pen, I was pleasantly surprised to see that Esperanza never tried to push into Stacy's space. Stacy continued to allow me to coach her as I continued to ask her body-centered questions. Stacy continued to be fully congruent by checking in with her body and sharing her anxiety, vulnerability, and agitation. She even once said, "I feel overwhelmed in my chest; there's so much energy moving through that area." Esperanza stood silently, holding the space beautifully for this young woman with red, curly hair to explore the different sensations moving in her body.

As Stacy continued to explore all of those different sensations, the more she became present with them. She understood that if she resisted the emotions in her body, they would only grow and fester and become more unmanageable. At that point, she would have no choice but to dissociate from them. She would be just like a horse who was pushed to the brink of what it could handle, engaging with coping mechanisms that could be dangerous to humans and cause accidents, such as rearing, running, or bolting.

Stacy continued to stand there mustering up all of her personal power to be fully present. As we dialogued Esperanza stood by her side. Her eyes were soft as if she was listening intently to our conversation. Stacy continued to be very genuine and real about what she was experiencing. At no time did this beautiful white mare with her big personality try to nip or be mouthy.

Stacy then began to mentalize her experience, and Esperanza walked away to the other side of the pen and sniffed the ground, basically ignoring us. I coached with Stacy, having her go deeper into this understanding of how hard it is for her to allow the energy to be present in her body and how she fears that if she allows herself to express herself, people will walk away. Just as Esperanza had. However, I pointed out to Stacy that Esperanza had been standing with us the entire time that she was focused on her body, and that Esperanza had never really left her when she was honest about her body. Esperanza only moved away from her when she began to doubt and mentalize what she was feeling, justify it, or try to understand it. That's when she lost Esperanza.

I worked with Stacy to help her realize the importance of staying true to herself. I asked her if she could create a sentence or phrase that would remind her how to stay with herself and remain present during the moments she wants to escape through mentalizing. I offered her phrases such as, "I'm worthy of being heard," "I'm worthy of being seen," "I am lovable." Stacy was a very good client. She was very receptive and would try each phrase out loud. She would say, "Yeah, that could work." Then, I would ask her, "Does it fit for you; is it really true for you?" She would say no to each one. I would encourage her to find what was true; what was her phrase? What was her statement that would help her always be herself; to never be affected by how someone responds to her? To always feel the strength and connection to herself first and foremost.

Then Stacy came up with the phrase, "I am unshakeable." As she said that statement, I watched Esperanza. She lifted her head and gave Stacy her very thoughtful eye. I knew in that moment that Stacy had nailed the correct statement. I asked Stacy to take some nice, deep breaths and to repeat this statement out loud while she walked toward Esperanza and to bring her awareness deep inside as she repeated her statement, "I am unshakeable."

Stacy proceeded to do so, and Esperanza watched her, her thoughtful eye gazing at her as Stacy began to walk around the round pen. When Stacy came up to Esperanza, there was no real interaction as they simply watched each other. And then Stacy decided to walk away, and I encouraged her to continue to say her statement out loud. "I am unshakeable." I could sense Stacy, out of the corner of her eye, watching Esperanza to see her reaction but bravely committed to her relationship with herself first, regardless of what another being did around her. Stacy fearlessly faced the possibility of rejection from the mare. She dropped more deeply into her statement, and I could hear the conviction of her voice. "I am unshakeable."

And then, Esperanza lifted her head fully up and began to follow Stacy, with her carrot-colored hair and her little sneakers and her sweet presence. Esperanza's footsteps came up behind her, and I could see the spark in Stacy's eyes when she realized the horse was following her. The tears welled up in her eyes, and big emotional tears fell down her cheeks. Stacy walked over to me, and Esperanza came right along by her side. Esperanza stood softly as she licked and chewed, never once entering into Stacy's space. Both of these beautiful, vibrant, intelligent beings with their big energies were in full communion with each other. I stepped back and away and invited Stacy to continue to commune with her new friend, the big, beautiful mare.

Stacy and I processed the experience along with Esperanza. Stacy realized that in all actuality when she stayed within herself while allowing herself to have big, sparkly, delightful energy, instead of another being leaving her, there was a high possibility they would join her just as Esperanza had. She knew she had been putting her attention on the wrong thing. She had been fearing being left behind so much that she'd left herself behind.

It's not uncommon for humans to abandon the emotional part of themselves. Often, it is the acceptance of the emotional part of ourselves that we most want to leave because emotions can bring discomfort to our bodies. We learn at a young age that emotions are not as accepted as we might want them to be when we're young. When we're young, we want to cry, rant, and declare things are unfair. But as we grow up, we are taught that little boys don't cry, and little girls don't get angry.

Stacy had reclaimed a part of herself that she had previously abandoned for the sake of being loved and included. She had decided that she could be comfortable in her body and that it was more important for her to allow herself to be big energetically to have all of the space she needed to self-express. Esperanza's reaction and response to that was a full honoring of Stacy. It was as if two big, beautiful, intelligent beings had come together to share and commune in their authentic way. Stacy found herself within the interaction with Esperanza.

As you reflect on this chapter, I encourage you to consider the following questions to find out if you may have left part of yourself behind or abandoned a part of yourself to conform and fit in. Many of us do this unconsciously but you'll seldom see horses do this; they will be exactly who they are as they find their place in the herd. They know their positions and they don't disqualify themselves or shrink to belong.

REFLECTIONS

Horses are authentic beings. They allow energy to move through them. They allow expression. They allow for whatever needs to arise in the moment, and then they go back to grazing. Wouldn't it be delightful if we could all do the same?

- What aspect of yourself do you tend to shrink or make small so that others will accept you? Where have you disowned part of your personality?
- When energy and emotion arise in your body, how do you deal with it? What would happen if you allowed yourself to be more present in your body without going into a coping strategy?

- Are you aware of when you are congruent and when you are incongruent? What are the results of your interactions when you are incongruent?
- What might it be like to acknowledge your feelings to yourself? Instead of trying to suppress your feelings, allow the beautiful emotions to move through you with grace.

Feel the Fear and Do It Anyway

Fear. It has the power to stop us in our tracks. Other times, our fear can be so intense that we want to fight back or run away. Sometimes it works subliminally to sabotage our dreams, our life path, and the possibility of living our passion. Fear can make us small.

The positive side of fear is that it keeps us physically, emotionally, and spiritually safe. Ask any person who has achieved any goal, and they will tell you how they worked with fear. At times they may have faced their fears and moved forward more boldly. Other times they heeded the profound message of fear and navigated a different direction or released the current engagement completely. Regardless of what you are trying to achieve, fear is an emotion to understand as you advance in life.

Fear is the same for horses. Horses are known for their propensity and tendency to be reactive and fearful. The majority of the time, the first reaction from a horse will be a startle and then run. Some react so quickly that they are instantly in flight. Their long legs and powerful bodies are designed to move them swiftly and rapidly out of danger and to a safe place.

Domesticated horses are conditioned to slow their natural and firmly embedded propensity to react through their training. If trained correctly, they can learn to control their impulses and think first. At the core of the horse's being (especially wild horses), this is counterintuitive to their way of being for thousands of years. Yet, for those who wish to use the horse for their work, pleasure, or competitive endeavors, the process of desensitizing a horse is crucial for the well-being of the rider and often also the horse.

Some domesticated horses are less lucky. Instead of having a trainer that understands the connection between the mind and body that can also help the horse learn new behaviors, the trainer intentionally or unintentionally teaches the horse to dissociate. These horses become so conditioned to the human's way that they respond to very little. Their eyes are often glazed over as if part of their free spirit is no longer inside of them because, in fact, it is not. They have learned to give their power to the rider and to tune out all of their sensing capabilities to survive the interactions they experienced in training. And the tuning out process continues throughout their life. They are robots, giving to man what he wants.

As many trainers and riding instructors will tell you, many fearful people want to be with horses. I was one of those people. I had to address my fears about horses before I could coach others. That process and my ability to use the coaching tools I developed helped me stay present with my fear while moving toward my goals. I had to resist every urge I had, just like a horse, and make myself think instead of reacting into a flight, fight, or freeze response.

One spring, I was in Belgium teaching on an old castle ground. The horse stables were in a square with the center paved in brick. The fruit trees were blooming, and the grass was coming up thick and tall. Birds were chirping and the skies were blue the entire time. I was leading a group of people through a Coaching with Horses program. A woman from France, Natalie, with little to no experience, admitted her fear about horses and her fear about stepping into the round pen while the horse was at liberty and could freely move wherever it pleased. She knew she wanted to include horses in her coaching and consulting work, yet she had to move through her fears and learn the skills needed to work with horses.

Having Natalie watch as many sessions as possible before placing her with a horse was important. It gave her time to understand how the horses move and the demeanor of the horses we were working with. My philosophy is to help build confidence one step at a time. She enjoyed watching the others, and I could see her anticipation building.

When it was her time, I set up many options for her. I let her know that it was her process and that she needed to take responsibility for the results of her experience. To help facilitate her integration and under-standing of fear, one of the options I offered was that I could work side by side with Natalie in a round pen session. I saw instant relief in her eyes when I suggested this, and she chose that option. The horse we worked with was a kind, gentle, yet flashy brown and white paint mare with one blue eye. Spirit was his name, and he was light on his feet.

Natalie heard me coach all of the other eight participants and had gained a visual of what happens in the round pen with a horse. She was able to observe the body language of the horses and the best position to be in when working with them. Additionally, I worked with everyone on how their thoughts and feelings and breath were affecting or influencing the results from the horses we worked with. Natalie had seen Spirit work with two other individuals, so she also had a sense of how he moved.

In all of my coaching with horses sessions, I focus strongly on help-ing people track their body sensations, emotions, and thought patterns. It was no different for Natalie. Since she was feeling fear, I needed to take these steps with her. I confirmed for her that she should be feeling fear, and that if she was not, I would be concerned. She was about to work with a thousand-pound animal who could move anywhere he wanted. She had never experienced this before and did not have the skills to know what to do. Her body was correct to tell her to be scared.

Spirit stood waiting patiently for us, and once I checked in with Natalie and made sure she felt prepared, we both walked in and moved to the center of the round pen. As we stood there, I continued to coach her while Spirit stood and watched. Natalie acknowledged her feelings, focused on her breath, articulated her fears, and allowed the stimulation in her body to come down as we talked about how safe we actually were. We were in the center of the pen and we both had carrot sticks. Outside of the round pen, I taught her how to create space around her by moving the stick. She also learned how to ask the horse to move out or change gaits with the stick.

As we stood there, I continued to teach her what to notice in Spirit's body. She learned how to observe if Spirit's eye was on us and if an ear was turned in toward us. She watched if his tail was relaxed. Spirit continued to stand and slowly started to lick and chew and yawn. This expression was biofeedback about my client's state of feeling.

With Natalie's hands on my hips, she followed right behind me as I started to work with Spirit. She was able to position her body correctly to communicate with him. Additionally, she was able to feel the energy of his movement while in the ring with me. I assured her that if he did decide to come into our space, I would keep a solid boundary with him. I was the barrier that gave her a sense of safety. I could sense her thinking, *Okay, he has to get past Kathy to get to me. I am safe.*

Of course, it was awkward, and I could sense her fumbling feet and short breath. Spirit kept his eye on us, truly entertained because I am sure he had never experienced this sort of thing before. We had him circle one way at a walk and light trot. Then he circled the other way. Slowly I sensed Natalie was starting to relax. She was walking more solidly, and her breath had lowered from her throat into her body.

We stopped and talked about all of it. I asked Natalie what she observed in Spirit's body. She had seen the changes he offered and when he was watching or looking away. We talked about her fear, and she admitted that she felt some anxiety and fear. However, it was not the same degree of fear that she had when she first came up to the round pen to start. I asked her if she was ready for her next step and reminded her again that she could call it quits whenever she wanted. She needed to know that she was not being forced to override her personal inner guidance system. Listening to her own fear, keeping her mind active, and not going into a flight, fight, or freeze mode was imperative.

I then had her stand beside me, and we put our arms around each other's waists. She was on the outside, or horse side, so she could use her carrot stick to signal the horse. I could also reach up with my arm to lower her arm if needed. Before we started to ask Spirit to move, I asked her to create a positive affirming phrase that would help her build her confidence. She chose, "It is safe to explore new things." I had her repeat this phrase several times as she also practiced deepening her breath. Once again, while standing and waiting patiently along the rail of our pen, Spirit turned his head, stared at us, and licked and chewed several times. Natalie and I observed the communication from him, with a demeanor soft and willing, and I could sense her relaxing even more.

Although somewhat awkward and clumsy, Natalie asked Spirit to move forward as I stayed by her side. Spirit was such a generous, kind horse, and I could see in his eye the understanding that this was not a traditional training experience. He comprehended her vulnerability and that she was learning. Not once was he defiant, rebellious, or attempting to take leadership and control. He indeed was a kind, sensitive horse.

Natalie moved him one way and then the other at a walk. She was learning about how her body position communicated to the horse and also how to properly use the carrot stick. Natalie, with a sparkle in her eyes, was talking with much more ease. She had more lightness in her step. As we stood in the center talking about what she had accomplished, Spirit let out a long breath and then began to bounce his head up and down as if to say, "Yes."

Natalie's last learning was to be in the front while I placed my hands on her hips and followed her around. I coached her as I followed from behind, giving tips, and correcting where I could to help her learn. Spirit continued to provide her more learning by resisting moving forward at first. Natalie had to bring up her energy and mean her request a bit more.

Eventually, I removed my hands as Natalie kept a good body position. I coached her more about how to place her focus and to notice things about Spirit's body language. When it was time to ask Spirit to move from a walk to a trot and then a light canter, I coached Natalie to use her breath as an indicator of pace change, along with her carrot stick. His flashy mane flowed behind him as he responded to each of her requests. He was relaxed, and so was Natalie. As they continued to move, I asked her to repeat her positive affirming statement out loud. She did so with a broad smile, lightness in her step, and a strong, straight back. Spirit reflected her state of clarity and commitment and desire to come from kindness. An authentic dance of communication unfolded. Gradually, Natalie moved from being my shadow to being by my side, and then, finally, to being in front working directly with Spirit on her own.

I admire Natalie for her ability to step into the round pen and acknowledge her feelings of fear, feel them, and continue to learn and achieve her life passion. Each time she progressed along the way, her fear diminished. She discovered that she had to take smaller baby steps when moving into something new. She had to learn to pay attention to her anxiety so that she could stay present in her mind to find success. Natalie also came to understand that when we want to grow, we often have to face fear head-on, that it is okay to have someone help, and that finding a kind teacher is vital.

Spirit was the perfect horse to teach Natalie. His contemplative nature quickly caught on to what we were doing. Because I was helping Natalie keep her attention on fear and trepidation, Spirit knew it was not something he had to react to. Horses like Spirit have so much to offer humans. So many times, their intelligence is missed because individuals are too busy and focused on how to achieve their goals with horses versus asking the horse how they want to give feedback. Spirit was a horse that had been trained to think. He was not a robot, and he did not mindlessly do what we wanted.

REFLECTIONS

How can Natalie's adventure with Spirit help you with your fears? What is the fear you most want to break free of? Take these steps to help you move through your anxiety of horses and any fear in your life:

- Assess the situation and know your limits. Trust the information from your body, but don't let it limit you! Be true to yourself about what you might need to feel safe. (*Natalie asked me to go with her into the round pen.*)

- Find a mentor who walked the path before you and can help you and coach you through your blocks. Be sure that your coach helps you integrate both the mind and the body so that your entire being is making lasting change. *(Natalie trusted me to help her.)*

- Access the feelings of fear in your body. Don't ignore fear. Keep conversing with the sensations and messages and build your sense of safety. This helps you to keep your center and stay in your power. (*Natalie was willing to pause and check in at all levels of her being.*)

- Gain knowledge. Learn about what you are engaging with so you have a strong base of knowledge and understanding. (*Natalie came to understand horses better.*)

- Stretch yourself. Acknowledge what is and decide what next small step you can take to get closer to your goal. (*Natalie moved from being my shadow to being by my side and, finally, in front of me.*)

Boundaries with a
Big Belgian Boy

Horses provide human beings the perfect opportunities to strengthen boundary-setting skills. As social animals, horses are always aware of each other and where they belong in the herd or family. Dynamics between horses are very fluid and changing. Some horses are more challenging than others; some horses give way to others. Many horses have an agenda with others in the herd. If they sense an opportunity to outsmart another horse to gain more status, by all means, they will step into that opportunity.

Part of gaining leadership in a herd is testing the boundaries of other herd mates. This testing is a natural process, especially when younger horses begin to grow into adults and feel more strength to experiment and push, becoming rebellious and outspoken, much like what we see teenagers do in high school. Everyone in the herd wants to feel a sense of belonging and being protected by the entire herd. A horse feels secure when she knows where she stands in the pecking order of the herd. To fully understand each other, they test limits. When a new horse arrives in the herd, eventually, she will integrate. She establishes herself in the pecking order by her ability to hold her boundaries and stand up to others when required.

When we engage with a horse, we enter into the natural herd dynamics they have with each other. One of the two individuals needs to take the lead, and if the human does not, the horse naturally will. They need answers to questions such as, who will respond if things get scary? Who will lead us to safety? Do I listen to you, or are you going to listen to me? When a horse understands where they belong in relationship to another, they feel safe. Even though the two beings officially do not create a herd, the dynamic is still there, and the questions require answers. Boundary work shows up in different ways for different people, including issues regarding personal space, operating from a heart-centered place versus the head, and making your voice heard. Each horse has its way of reflecting to the person what boundary issues need addressing.

Once during a cold northern winter, I headed south to teach with horses in Tucson, Arizona. The skies were a soft light blue, and rain the previous days had left the arena dust-free. In the early morning, the smell of mesquite filled the air. The cacti were just beginning to bloom with yellows and reds, and the birds were happily moving about to the fresh nectar as the temperature rose. The day was perfect to be playing with horses, not too hot or too cold, and there was no wind. The horses seemed content. The horses always love it when I bring programs to the dude ranch; it is something different than taking people on their backs through the same sandy and rocky trails of the desert. With my clients and me, they can use their minds and be creative.

Evelyn, a therapist from North Carolina, came to the personal development program I was offering. Soft-spoken, she often sat with her eyes gazing downward, avoiding visual contact with others in the group. Evelyn was extremely kind and very sensitive to others and the larger group; she was well put together and nonthreatening. And yet, many in the group had not connected with her.

Evelyn was preparing to work with a substantial Belgian horse by the name of Rawhide. Belgian drafts were initially bred to be workhorses.

Their easy temperaments and broad, muscular bodies made them perfect partners to plow fields or haul wagons filled with lumber or food. Bred to be thicker and more durable, Belgians could perform the heavy workload that, at the time, engines were not available to do. The modern Belgian draft horse is still significant in size and often used to pull carts. In adulthood, they can reach the weight of two thousand pounds and stand up to, and sometimes over, seventeen hands high. Because of their easygoing nature, they have become pleasure-riding horses. Many dude ranches in the western states employ draft horses, as these horses can more easily handle heavy riders.

Rawhide, only five years old at the time, was at least sixteen hands high and still growing. His hooves were the size of large dinner plates. He was a beautiful medium-tan color, just like rawhide leather. His light blonde mane, tail, feathers at his hooves, and forelocks that hung over his eyes brought an element of innocence to his appearance in contrast to his massive body. Most people, including myself, first responded to this horse by wanting to hug him. He looked like an oversized, gentle teddy bear.

Evelyn felt the same way. She immediately fell in love with him and could not take her eyes off him. She looked at him more than she looked at anyone in the group. She was excited at the possibility of working with him.

We had spent the morning talking about all the nuances of boundaries. In the human world, understanding that boundaries are physical and also emotional, spiritual, and mental can be surprising for many. That was not true for Evelyn; after all, she was a therapist and claimed that she had done her boundary work. But once Evelyn was in the round pen with Rawhide, everything changed. Being a curious and playful young horse,

Rawhide brought his massive body right over to Evelyn and wanted to engage with her. He had not had a lot of training on the ground and, indeed, very little natural horsemanship training. He had only been at the ranch for a few months. He was not aggressive or mean; instead, he was sweet. He also was curious and wanted to engage with Evelyn, just like he did all of his other herd mates. To him, she was just another horse.

Evelyn had also indicated that she had a fair amount of horse experience. She had two at home, and she had been to the ranch several times to enjoy trail riding. Through the years, I have learned that how people express the amount of horse experience they have is very personal to their perspective. Having had clients who claimed to have expert knowledge tie a horse's lead line to the bottom rung of a steel piped fence, I never believe what people say. Instead, I watch and immediately know who they are, what kind of boundaries they own, and what type of horse experience they have. I do not judge if they appear to be a more passive or more aggressive communicator with a horse; I simply observe and wait for the horse to present the teaching for the day.

As you are already sensing, the session did indeed become about setting boundaries. In Rawhide's case, the work was about physical boundaries. From my description above, you may have conjured up an image of Evelyn being a petite, thin, or frail woman, one who does not take up much space visually. The opposite is true. Evelyn is five-ten in height. She is by no means model thin, nor is she overweight. One might refer to her physical appearance as large-boned. In reality, she is of average weight.

When Rawhide approached her, he immediately went right up to connect with her, his large hooves only inches from her now-dwarfed size nine boots. His teddy bear head loomed over the top of hers. I took a deep breath and thought to myself, *Okay, here we go, let the boundary-setting session begin.*

I asked Evelyn if she was comfortable with how close her horse was. She replied yes, with hesitation in her voice. I asked her if she was telling the truth, while I also kept an eye on her beautiful leather boots. She paused. I asked her how well she knew this horse. Did she know him well enough to have him in her personal space? With a challenging tone in my voice, I asked her to speak her truth. Finally, with Rawhide still right next to her and his head above her, she said maybe a little more space might be helpful. I suggested that she create a boundary with him just as she would with one of her horses at home. Gently, she placed her hand on his chest and gave a little pressure. More than likely, her horses at home comply and back up with that pressure. Not Rawhide. He probably experienced her hand and the pressure she was applying as a sweet comfort.

Clients often struggle with setting appropriate boundaries with horses. I have watched horses get into a person's personal space (a three-foot space that surrounds the physical body) and then nudge or push the person to establish hierarchy, be playful, or to test. The person, unaware of what is happening, will often unconsciously take a step back. Rawhide responded precisely in this way, taking the lead and moving as close as he could to Evelyn without stepping on her. She unconsciously stepped back.

As the coach, I had to up my game. Evelyn needed to pay attention to her personal space, including her feet; otherwise, Rawhide could unintentionally step on her, which would be a disaster. I asked her to bring up more energy and truly set a boundary with the horse. I told her Rawhide needed to be at least three feet away from her if not five feet. I told her she needed to have more intention in applying pressure with her hand and to look back behind him, not at her own feet. She tried again and failed. Rawhide now was beginning to nuzzle her reddish-brown hair, and they were visually beginning to blend.

I shared with Evelyn that she might be enjoying this intimate exchange with Rawhide, but it could quickly escalate, as he was viewing her as another horse. I told Evelyn to move to safety at the center of the round pen. I instructed her to use the carrot stick that lay on the ground to set her space and boundary with Rawhide as we had practiced earlier in the day. Reluctantly, she did. Rawhide, of course, did not miss a beat. Slowly he shifted his massive body and took slow, heavy steps toward her. Evelyn picked up the stick, and I coached her to set the boundary. She was slow with her command, Rawhide kept coming, and eventually, Evelyn stepped backward out of his way yet again.

Between you and me, sessions like this thrill me. I love allowing my coaching to get enough fire behind it to support a person in setting their space. What I love the most about it is that the person always has to access a suppressed part of their personality and reserves of strength to do so. Evelyn was no different.

While Rawhide once again was too close to her, I began to coach Evelyn. I asked her key questions such as, "How comfortable are you right now? What might happen if you allow him to continue? What will it take for you to step it up and demand what you need and want? When have you been able to set boundaries before?" And my favorite question, "What do you need to believe to have your space respected?"

Through this dialogue, Evelyn would answer a question and wave her stick at the same time. Rawhide just kept walking toward her, and Evelyn kept walking backward. Eventually, Evelyn identified that she believed she did not feel she had the right to have her space. I helped her create a powerful statement to change that belief and improve her experience with Rawhide.

Her statement was: I have the right to have my own space. I asked her to walk away from Rawhide, turn around, and use her new belief statement as he approached this time. She went halfway to the other side of the pen. Once again, Rawhide lumbered over, lazily dragging his large feet. He was in no rush and seemed to be enjoying the game.

I coached her to start saying her statement out loud as she used her carrot stick to signify the line as she waved it in front of her. Rawhide kept coming. My energy increased as I coached her like a football coach would coach his player. "Say it like you mean it, Evelyn. Come from your belly. Use all of your energy. Do *you* believe it, Evelyn? Do *you* believe you have the right to your space? I can't hear you, Evelyn! I don't believe you! Own it! Own it in your body."

As you can imagine, time moves fast in these moments. Evelyn caught the heat of the fire behind my words, and she finally lit up with more determination. Finally, just as Rawhide was about five feet away, there was a shift in Evelyn. Her body got stronger, her voice deepened, and the words resonated with truth for the first time since we had started. Rawhide stopped. He hung his head down softly and began to lick and chew. As he relaxed, I could sense the wheels in his mind turning with understanding. As I looked at Evelyn, I could sense an entirely new way of being and believing in her abilities integrating into her body. She had set a successful boundary with an enormous animal.

Evelyn and Rawhide stood staring at each other, each of them digesting the lesson they learned. Rawhide learned what it felt like to have a human set a boundary with him. Evelyn got to experience the power of claiming her space with Rawhide and in the world. Rawhide quietly and respectfully stood as Evelyn and I talked. She was able to explore where she had not done well with setting boundaries. She realized that often she let others in too quickly when she was attracted to them for whatever reason. She said that in her practice, her clients would often start to ask for more and more of her time. She had a hard time getting them to leave the office. The more she processed, the more she realized just how much she gave her time and emotional presence to others, often to her own detriment.

Evelyn's ability to access and evoke the emotions of frustration and anger through her body helped her have more determination in setting her boundary. Once she was fully present and congruent in her body and mind, she created momentum, alignment, and a more definite intention. Evelyn did not lash out at Rawhide. Instead, she had one hundred percent clarity in her expression. That is when the boundary became successful.

The visceral experience of setting a boundary with a fifteen-hundred-pound horse brings individuals to new levels of personal power. This newly established strength quickly transfers into everyday life and interactions with people. Boundary setting becomes more natural and less fearful. People begin to hear and respect their requests. With horses, we learn how to set proper boundaries in the areas of our heart, home, physical and emotional well-being, and our spirituality.

Boundaries are not walls, but standards for right behavior and action for you and those around you to honor. Everyone has different requirements for boundaries and often at different times. You set a boundary when a person or horse comes toward you. A person or a horse sets a limit when you approach them. Your horse will tell you every time you approach her where her boundary is; your job is to watch and listen for the signs (ears flicking, an eye on you, the swish of a tail, a ripple through the skin). Once a horse expresses her boundary, simply pause and take a breath. This demonstrates that you understand her subtle communication, and that you respect her request. Then, say hello and slow down before you approach her again, always paying attention to how she communicates through body language.

Where you feel others trespass your boundaries, you are usually transgressing the same boundary with others. Boundaries honor your spirit and sense of self, and the correct application of boundary setting will often increase respect and trust in relationships and renew your energy. Highly sensitive people and horses can disappear or dissociate during stressful interactions with others. Both can heal and then naturally flourish and grow when their boundaries are defined, acknowledged, and respected. Anger often indicates that a boundary has been crossed. When you feel shame, you may have crossed someone else's boundary.

Think of boundaries as a dance of understanding. You are respecting the limits in relationships with your horses and your friends and family. The line can move at times, and the dance is ongoing. What is most important is that you are clear about what you need, you take responsibility to communicate those needs clearly, and you pay attention to others' needs without unconsciously sacrificing your own.

REFLECTIONS

Boundaries set with firm, compassionate, body-centered communication that exudes power, will, and respect convey a clear and direct message that a horse and another person respond to with cooperation. In the dance of understanding boundaries, clarity of your internal and external needs combined with clear communication are essential.

- Where have you not been clear in your needs and desires?
- How can you change your communication without amplifying your emotions or covering them up to pacify others?
- What would change in your life if you set clear and understandable boundaries with your horses and other people?
- How can you say yes and still have a clear boundary?

The Big Man and Little Lulu

From thirty thousand feet in the air, I pressed my face against the airplane window as I strained to see the mountainous terrain below me. The clouds came and went, and when they cleared, I could see the vibrant green mountains with deep ravines and powerful rivers running through them.

As we began our descent, I noticed all of the mountainsides were sprinkled with small houses and many of them with large greenhouses. I mentioned this to the man who sat next to me. The plane was full due to a cancellation the night before, and after many hours stuck in the Miami airport, I considered myself lucky to finally be on the plane. The man was a wholesale flower buyer from Belgium, and we began to talk about how the country of Colombia is one of the largest suppliers of flowers in the world. As we descended, I noticed more and more large greenhouses. Coming from Colorado where the climate is dry, I was excited to experience the lush, warm climate of Colombia with the cool nights and slight rain showers.

When we finally landed, my hosts Aldo, Catalina, and David greeted me. I was relieved to embrace all of them. They were so happy to see me, and they filled me with joyous bubbling energy after the hardship of travel. We headed off to the countryside outside the city of Medellin.

Colombia is not a place I had ever set out to visit. When Aldo first joined my certification class, on day two he asked me to come to

Colombia to share in the beautiful interaction with horses around the city of Medellin. I put him off because my first reaction was uncertainty about traveling to a country that had been through so much history. I needed some time to digest the idea and feel into whether it was the best place for me to go. And now I was there.

My hosts whisked me from the airport to Bambusa, an elegant, restful piece of property. The rolling hills surrounding the estate were lush and green. Beautiful architecture integrated the land and the outside into the actual home. The house had large sliding glass doors that opened to a green garden of herbs, flowers, and cacti. Even when the glass doors were shut, you still felt like you were outside. A water feature created a gentle stream down an outside wall of the house that poured into a long rectangular pool otherwise filled with still water. A small pathway guided me through a variety of vegetation in a pattern designed by the owner's wife. I found the setting deeply peaceful.

The arena was the most beautiful I'd ever seen. Tilted rooflines created interesting shadows on the floor of the arena. It was all open-air with big beams, steel framework, and gorgeous woodwork. It was top of the line, a perfect setting. The entire property was by far the most luxurious place I'd traveled to in all my years of doing this work. I'd been to Australia, Canada, Germany, Belgium, the Netherlands, and Spain. I'd traveled all over the world and had never experienced such a refined setting for exploring with horses.

The patron of Bambusa, Carlos, had a very still and calm presence. He was very composed and well put together, just like his property. He was already a well-known leader. I wondered what teachings the horses would offer him and all of the people he had personally invited to attend. Carlos was a thinker and a kind man respected by all who knew him.

Aldo had told me that I'd be working with some of the highest levels of leaders in the country, men who ran companies with a thousand or more employees, the bigger, larger companies of the country. It was a realm in which I'd never spent much time. Being able to stay on this property and be part of the atmosphere he'd created and get to know him and his horses was a treat beyond words.

I enjoyed the first evening getting to know everyone and sharing a meal on the outdoor patio, watching as the sun set ever so slowly and gently in the night air. The day had cooled as the night came upon us as I sipped a tea infused with several fresh herbs from the garden. The next day would be long because I'd lost a full day due to the canceled flight, so we made our plan, and I went off to get a good night's sleep.

After breakfast, I went out to meet all of the horses so I could see which horses would be most appropriate to work with the arriving guests. There were seven horses on the property, including two that were Carlos's riding horses imported from Belgium. They were beautiful warm-blooded horses of the most refined level. Carlos had been riding all of his life, and his preferred style of riding was dressage. He was a very disciplined man, and so dressage worked very well for him, as it is a disciplined method of riding.

I let Aldo know that the first thing we'd have to do when I arrived was bring all of the horses into the arena. Mind you, Carlos's horses came into the arena every week because they were ridden quite often. They were used to being under the arena roof and being in that atmosphere, but we introduced two new round pen areas which were new to them. I always like to make sure that the horses are comfortable in the areas we are going to explore so they can be more present to the people who are engaging with them. I needed to see which horses were bound to the herd and which ones were comfortable being away from the others.

In the brilliant green pasture under powder-blue skies and puffy white clouds were two warmbloods, a beautiful brownish-colored horse, a lighter-colored quarter horse—and a very small white and black paint mini. What a surprise she was. The day of exploration with these horses was very adventurous. We would place one horse in one round pen and another in another round pen and wait for their response as we let them go at liberty. They were free to roll, run, and buck. Whatever expression they needed to do, they could do in the round pen to get out their energy and be more present the next day when the program started.

Watching all of these horses and their personalities to see how each of them responded and to find out which were not comfortable with their partners being taken away was fascinating. The horse that captured me more than the large warmbloods and the beautiful calm mare, the one that took me by surprise, was Lulu, the black and white mini-horse. Carlos told me the story of all his horses' backgrounds and stories so I could get a sense of where they may have come from and how that might play out with my clients.

In telling me about Lulu, Carlos said that he came home from work one day and was getting ready to ride his horse when a float (horse trailer) pulled up. Out of the float came Lulu. Carlos was bewildered because he had no idea where the horse came from. His wife, Esperanza, decided on a whim to rescue this horse and bring her to their property, so off went little Lulu to become part of the larger herd of warmbloods and other full-sized riding horses.

We put Lulu into the round pen, and I saw all of the feistiness that a mini-horse could have. As I entered into the round pen, she had lots of things to say. I asked her to back up and give me some space, and off around the round pen she went running, her little legs pounding in the sand as her mane blew back behind her. She charged up to me again, and I said, "I don't think so," and asked her to get back to the rail to create more space around me.

I gave her a little bit of energy, and she gave me a lot of energy back. She bucked and kicked, running around with all sorts of opinions to express. Back and forth we went for a while, and eventually, her energy started to calm down. When she came into me, she respectively listened to the space I needed. Even when she initially respected my space, I could feel in my bones that if I let my awareness go somewhere else, she would come right back into my bubble and possibly start to nibble on me or kick up her heels and do something naughty. She'd already shown signs of this behavior.

I wasn't sure if this horse would be appropriate for me to use in the program. I had been told that many of the participants coming in either owned horses or donkeys or had been around horses before because horses are prevalent in the country, used for working the land or for pleasure riding. Carlos and I discussed using Lulu quite a bit, and then I asked him if he'd like to go in and work with her since he had not previously gotten to know her well. Carlos, in his very earthy, quiet way, entered into the round pen. Lulu came up, and Carlos simply put his hands up and said no. Lulu pushed that boundary, and Carlos said no again. He did it very quietly and very gently. She pushed more, and he very gently put his hand on her. I could tell he was having a little bit of an exchange with her, and then he asked her again to give him space. That time, she complied. Carlos worked with her a little bit in the round pen, and her feistiness diminished. It was as if she knew that he was the patron of the property and she needed to behave with him versus when I played with her. She had no idea who I was, she had never seen me before.

Carlos and I chatted about it, and I told him I'd have to think about whether I could use Lulu because I was not sure how she would do with someone who had little experience or who was afraid and would go to dominance as an approach if frightened. All the other horses seemed entirely appropriate, and I was very taken by all of them. They had even temperaments, and they were very kind. Some had higher energy than others, but I could tell right away which would be good teachers. I was skeptical about the dressage horses; I was not one hundred percent sure I wanted to use them. I knew that the other horses were used less so naturally I gravitated toward working with them.

By the end of the day, I told Aldo and Carlos that we would use all of the horses except for Lulu. She was much too opinionated and boisterous and had too much fire in her. I did not feel safe using her. We all agreed that would be fine, and Aldo assured me he would get the horses' written history so we could talk to the clients about them.

We had a full day exploring with the horses and, of course, that put a big smile on my face. I love introducing the work to them, and I always stop with each of the horses and have a silent exchange with them. In those moments, I stand quietly with them, I take a few deep breaths, and I allow my sensory awareness to open up. I come into their time. I tell them in mind or softly speaking aloud about what we are going to be doing the next day. I invite them to become teachers for humans, to be a horse, and do what horses naturally do, even around the humans that will work with them. I tell each of them that I know they have a lot of wisdom to share, and this is their opportunity to teach humans. I then hold a vision of my horses in Colorado in round pens showing different things a horse can do to teach while standing on the ground with a person. I let them know that they are being given an opportunity to express things that maybe they have not expressed before. It is a very pleasurable experience for me to have this exchange and conversation with horses that I do not know. I implicitly trust that horses understand my communication through words and visuals. They come to realize what I represent, and that I'm standing for the wisdom horses have for humans.

We retired for the evening and had a lovely meal before doing the program's last preparations. I was anxious to sleep because I was exhausted from the evening I'd spent in the airport. Instead, I tossed and turned, and every time I woke up, the name Lulu would crash into my mind. After three or four times hearing her name, I finally said, "Okay, fine. I hear you, Lulu. I know you want to come and play, so leave me alone so I can sleep." After that, I was able to sleep soundly for three hours before sunrise. When I woke, I kept my commitment to Lulu. When I sat down for breakfast, I told Aldo and Carlos that Lulu had come to me in the night, and she needs to be in this program, in fact, that she insisted she be part of it.

We made the change and included her in the program. I was secretly wondering how this would turn out. But, after doing so many programs throughout the world for the past fifteen years, I know that when the horses speak to me in my dreams, I have to listen and follow their lead. Into the program Lulu went, and now we had a herd of six.

The group that formed the next morning was a beautiful group of many leaders in the country. There were well-known executives and forward-thinking individuals, along with young people starting new schools or projects who were very socially oriented. Everyone had an interest in becoming better leaders; such a joyful experience for me. As I sat in a circle with the group, I talked extensively about why we used horses as teachers. I talked about how horses do leadership, about leadership itself. Observing how all of these people who were listening to me were so sincere and intense was fascinating. All of them spoke Spanish but also spoke English. The energy in the group was so receptive and so caring, I felt embraced and respected instantly. The feeling for me was very warm and overwhelming because often when I've traveled, I've met resistance or competition. This group was wide open. I asked them all sorts of questions around leadership, and it was interesting to see some of their responses.

The first activity we did was called "observe the herd," where we simply took the participants out to observe the dynamics within the herd. We sat in silence, observing for about thirty minutes. When we gathered back in the group, I asked many questions that would help them understand what they had seen, what sort of interactions were going on between different horses, and why those interactions were happening. Finally, we explored who the leader of the herd really was. It fascinated me to hear why people chose different horses as the leader because it revealed to me what their concept of a leader was.

One said they liked the kind mare and thought she was the leader because she was very subtle in her communication but would separate horses when they were starting to get rambunctious and did not seem fazed by a lot of different things. Another individual said he couldn't identify any leader, as if the herd did not have a leader, that one did not seem more prominent than another. Interestingly, as we discovered, one of the horses had been taken out of the herd and brought into the barn due to an injury. Just a week before I arrived, another horse had been taken out of the herd. The herd was currently in a reorganizational phase where not one horse stood out as the leader. The individual who shared this observation was the person with the least amount of horse experience, and I found that utterly fascinating.

One man stood out to me, Pedro Miguel. He seemed a little rougher around the edges and spoke very directly. I found myself rather curious about him. He thought that the bully was the leader. He identified that the horse going around and nipping and creating friction in the herd was in charge. When I asked him why he thought it was that horse, he said because that horse was more dominant, so that was why he was the leader of the herd.

The group had wonderful in-depth conversations about leadership and horses and the relationship of the leader with the others in the herd. They learned that the most dominant horse in the herd is not the leader. In fact, the most dominant horse in the herd is not always respected. A dominant horse does sometimes create order and disorder but is not usually considered the absolute leader. We talked about how often there are two leaders in wild herds: a mare and a stallion, and about the different ways that a mare leads compared to a stallion. We talked about the different purposes of leadership within a herd: to keep predators or other stallions away from the family herd in the wild; to find food and water; to nurture and maintain a cohesive community within the family. Both the mare and the stallion play many different roles.

These conversations challenged the group's perceptions of what leadership was and how we maintain relationships and heart-centered connections within our leadership. I could hardly wait to get these kind, gentle, open individuals out to work with the horses. I knew that the horses would teach them some very important lessons.

In the afternoon, we gathered at the arena. I'd paired all of the participants with the horses that they felt most drawn to work with. Pedro Miguel, the man who had picked the most dominant horse to be the leader, interestingly picked little Lulu. I thought this was going to be a very interesting interaction and could hardly wait for it to begin.

The arena felt very spacious. The sand was clean and smooth, and we had placed Lulu in the arena. Pedro Miguel and I stood in the middle of the arena, and we talked about what he might focus on with Lulu. Given that I'd already seen Lulu's behavior with Carlos and myself, I anticipated how she might behave with Pedro Miguel. But I had also learned in my fifteen years of doing equine facilitated learning never to make assumptions; each horse will respond to each person differently according to whatever energy, emotion, and intention the human offers them in the moment.

Pedro Miguel and I approached Lulu. His instruction was to approach and see if he could motivate the horse to keep her space from his space, meaning he'd have to hold his ground with her. As he started to approach Lulu, she came directly forward to him. I followed closely behind, anticipating what might transpire. Lulu came right up into Pedro Miguel's space. He would use the carrot stick and wave his arms to keep her out of his space. He even became a little bit dominant, a little more aggressive with the whip. Yet Lulu was persistent; she wasn't going anywhere. I knew that Lulu also had the propensity to get nippy. I think she'd gotten away with a lot of bad behavior because of her smaller size. She definitely had things to say and made it very clear overnight that she needed to be a part of this program. I trusted the process and the exchange that was beginning to happen between Pedro Miguel and Lulu, and also stayed on my toes to prevent any nips or kicks from happening.

As I approached Pedro Miguel, I began to dialogue with him and asked him how he felt about Lulu and the space she was encroaching. He said that he preferred her not to be in his space, but he found her cute, and although he was quite persistent in asking her to get out, she was not listening. I also noticed that he began to reach down and try to caress her, giving Lulu a mixed message. Pedro Miguel and I discussed this as Lulu stood still watching the exchange between us, first her eyes on me and then her eyes on Pedro Miguel. She was a cute little horse, really, but I knew what she was capable of.

Pedro Miguel was very familiar with horses, yet with everyone watching, this little horse was teaching him a lesson he was not expecting. He had never experienced a horse teaching him; he had always been more dominant in his relationships with horses. As Pedro Miguel and I began to talk, he revealed to me that he was head of a company of over one thousand employees. He was very proud of his company; it was his life's work, and he knew the name of every employee who worked for him. He was a loving and caring leader, but his feedback from others was that he was too dominant, similar to how he acted with Lulu. It pained him that this behavior would come out of him and he didn't know how to resolve it. He felt a lot of pressure to run a successful company. As he spoke and shared some of his stories, I gathered that he was a very generous man. He told me how they had lost one of their employees to the mafia, and it had been a very tough time for him and his company. He mentioned that he cared for his employees and had pride in knowing each of their names.

I sensed the big heart of this man, and although he appeared to be rough around the edges, inside he was a wonderful, warm, loving, and caring person who strived to do well by others. As he shared more stories of what happened to his employees, Lulu stood still and watched us. Pedro Miguel mentioned how often he would give so much to his employees, but eventually some would start to take or ask even more of him. That is when he would snap and become upset, defensive, and push others away.

As he began to speak this truth, Lulu's head dropped down, and she began to lick and chew. I knew what Pedro Miguel was sharing was of the utmost importance; this was the truth of what caused his abrupt and abrasive behavior and why he would lose his temper. I spoke with Pedro Miguel about boundaries and explained that his job in this exercise was to keep Lulu out of his space. Lulu was still in his space. I talked with Pedro Miguel about how having a big heart and sharing all that he has is a wonderful attribute to offer others but it is also important to maintain and respect his own emotional needs and requirements. Giving is okay, but giving too much drains the leader's energy, and those who follow lose respect when the leader becomes unexpectedly prickly or harsh. As I shared this information with Pedro Miguel, I noticed his eyes changed. There was a softening, and I could sense the emotion building within him. He acknowledged that, yes, this was true. He loved everyone so much and wanted to do so much for them that he would often not take care of himself.

Lulu continued to stand, licking and chewing here and there. Pedro Miguel and I discussed this concept further. I asked him what it might be like to know when he was about to give too much. He needed to honor his generous heart at the same time he established and sustained strong boundaries. He agreed that it would be a worthy thing to explore. He admitted that since he was young, he had always given more than paying attention to his own needs. I asked him what would be an inner voice he could put into place to help establish his personal space and needs in relationship to others as a leader of a very large company.

The voice he came up with was, "I can lead with firm boundaries and kindness." As he said that, Lulu once again began to lick and chew. I love the instant feedback that this little horse was giving Pedro Miguel.

I mentioned to him the behavior that Lulu was demonstrating, and if he knew its significance. He said he'd noticed it, and we discussed how her energy was beginning to calm, and she was processing the exchange he and I were having. I asked him if he would be willing to set different limits at this moment to embrace and embody the power of his leadership through firm boundaries and kindness. He was hesitant to try this out, and I sensed that it was probably his awareness of being watched by others.

We continued, and I asked him to repeat his voice, breathe deep into his body, and see Lulu as being some of the members of his organization with whom he could have better boundaries. He took a few breaths and repeated his statement out loud, and ever so gently he asked Lulu to move out of his space by waving the carrot stick in front of her. She just looked at him inquisitively. I could sense that the gentle giant before me did not want to be cruel to this tiny horse. He wanted to be fair. He wanted to be a good leader in this horse's eyes, in the eyes of everyone watching, and most importantly, through his own eyes. I asked him to bring up his energy again and I could see him shift his body slightly and breathe deeper into his chest and belly. He was intent now on accomplishing this task. Once again, he said his statement, and he waved the carrot stick. Lulu very slowly and precisely took two steps back.

Then, Pedro Miguel sighed. I could see the beginning of tears forming in his eyes. I came to understand that Pedro Miguel's world was about helping others, but when pushed to his limits, his only way of coping was to push back and become harsher with others. This behavior is not uncommon in a herd of horses. One horse might become complacent and put up with a lot from the others. They might be docile and have weaker boundaries, allowing others to come in and take their food or move them away from water. They'll live that way for a certain amount of time, and then one day, their response will be dramatic, and they will retaliate against the herd member. Typically, the other herd members will be surprised and often comply with that horse's desires, intuitively understanding that there has been imbalance all along.

The difference between horses and humans is that horses will go back to grazing with no judgment after such an incident. In the human world, when a person behaves like this, they are often judged as being an aggressor. The individual who has performed such acts often feels shame for the behavior that came forward as a natural defense mechanism. Imagine how things would be different if we as humans could learn how to stand our ground more securely in our leadership with others.

For Pedro Miguel, the day was a game-changer. He came to understand that leadership is not about aggression. He also came to understand that it is not about giving everyone everything they need at all times. The thing missing for him was that he needed to respect the amount of time and energy and space he could give to others so that he wouldn't go to the extreme of being aggressive to set his boundaries.

The little black and white mini-horse stood there staring at him intently as he voiced his realizations. The moment was heartwarming and made me realize how powerful every horse in this world is, regardless of shape, size, color, or breed. Every being in this world is a mirror for us to learn how to become more conscious in our interactions and relationships.

I, too, had learned my lessons from Lulu. I learned how to be a better leader, just as Pedro Miguel had. Additionally, I learned that in being a leader, one must also listen to their intuition and trust their gut feelings about what needs to transpire for the community. I had honored that Lulu came to me in my dreams, waking me in the night so many times, so I knew she would be a part of the program. She taught this man a wonderful lesson that would allow him to be an even better leader, because he learned how to take better care of his boundaries and needs within relationships. It's a lesson we can all learn.

REFLECTIONS

Little Lulu proved to be an incredible teacher, an unexpected delight for all those who interacted with her. When I finally left, I was deeply touched by all that had transpired on the beautiful property. But more than anything else, I was deeply touched by the kindness, receptivity, and openness of the people I met. In all of the countries I've visited, I've never experienced the open, heart-centered connection I experienced in Colombia.

I was also deeply touched by how quickly all of the horses stepped so quickly into this unique way of teaching humans. Every year, it seems that more horses on the planet understand that they can be heard, considered, and recognized as teachers for mankind. For those people who wish to listen to them in this way, there is a mutually beneficial experience where growth can happen for all, and in that growth, also wellness.

- How can you be a better leader for your horse? For your family? For your business?
- What can Lulu's story teach you about expectations?
- What can your horse teach you about boundaries?
- Have you been clear about your boundaries, or do you often give too much, then feel resentful or exhausted?
- Have you respected and honored other beings' boundaries?
- What can you do to set clearer and more beneficial boundaries?

From Peacemaker to Living Life Fully

A woman named Judy came to work with the horses and me to improve her leadership skills. She was a petite woman who ran a very successful creative agency out of New York City. Bright, energetic, thoughtful, and very savvy with her social intelligence, I was excited to work with her. I had no doubt that she would learn something. What transpired was powerful and deeply cathartic for her.

Judy chose to work with Ginger, the youngest in my herd and a spunky, responsive, and curious horse. Ginger had little fear, and I sensed that someday she would rise to be a lead mare like her mother. Ginger had received a lot of training, starting just a few weeks after she was born. She was brave, intelligent, and sometimes a bit pushier and more forward than I liked, but very aware of another's personal space. She knew that when a person raised their hands in front of them or waved a tool called a carrot stick, it meant she should stop and respect the human's request for space.

However, in the teaching sessions with horses, the horses are at liberty. They are given the freedom to respond to a person from the horse's perspective, and as a result, they often become a mirror of the human's consciousness. How they respond is where the teaching for the human begins. When a human joins a horse in a defined area, the horse wants to know who will lead.

As a high-powered business owner, Judy had many people she man-aged and a lot of responsibilities on her plate. I intuitively sensed that Ginger might challenge Judy. However, I was unsure what that would bring up since I experienced Judy as a very respectful person of other people's needs and personal space. I was prepared to coach my client to own her space if this endearing, precocious little four-year-old horse challenged her. Secretly, I was rather excited to do so because I knew how this exercise could ignite a person to declare an aspect of themselves that they may have lost along the journey of life. The work can be life changing.

Every true leader needs the skill of their conviction, communication, and power. However, I have discovered throughout the many years of working with people that most leaders will find holes in their leadership style when placed with a thousand-pound horse. Many leaders have huge hearts, but often have poor boundary-setting skills. Other leaders may lead from fear, keeping their authenticity tucked away. Some leaders can be people pleasers, never really speaking their full truth. The gifts and teachings a horse can provide for leaders are endless.

I prepared Judy outside the round pen by helping her bring aware-ness into her body to sense the environmental influences through her five senses. She then focused on her heart space, offering words of apprecia-tion to Ginger. Judy found Ginger to be playful, daring, courageous, and mischievous. Judy declared she wanted to be able to "play" with Ginger. Judy was ready to dive into the relationship.

Centered in her heart space, Judy moved into the round pen area with Ginger. After Judy approached Ginger to connect and say hello, she then asked her to move around the round pen. Ginger willingly went along. Like most horses, she questioned who was going to be in charge and be the leader. Instead of complying and staying on the round pen's outer edge, Ginger began to come closer to Judy. Essentially, she was squeezing and filling the space between them. Judy started to use the carrot stick to ask Ginger to stop coming into her space. I could see the shift in Judy's body from a relaxed state to more tension. Her shoulders rounded a bit as her posture shrunk. Ginger, too, could see and sense the change in Judy. The holes in Judy's leadership were about to emerge.

Horses will follow the individual who demonstrates the calmest presence and highest sense of confidence. The bully of the herd or the member showing dominance is not the true leader. Ginger could sense the trepidation in Judy and attempted to take the lead with her bold forward energy. Ginger was simply exploring the relationship. Ginger's behavior was a way of asking questions of Judy to see if she could indeed lead. I read Ginger's questions to be: *Are you in your body? Do you really know where your personal space is? Can you stand your ground with me? Can you access the level of power I need to trust your leadership? Are you a pushover? And who will lead between the two of us? What is our relationship going to be about?*

Ginger's body language continued to demonstrate her questioning as she approached Judy without stopping. Judy held the carrot stick, then waved the carrot stick, then waved it with more determination, and yet Ginger kept moving toward her. Eventually, Ginger was in Judy's personal space. The stimulation of Ginger's energy as she moved around and the energy exerted as Judy attempted to gain her own space became too much for her. Judy's body melted into a heap of disappointment and despair.

I stepped up my coaching with Judy and helped her see that she was technically doing all of the right things. However, the energy of her conviction was not present. Little Ginger could sense that Judy was not entirely committed to her endeavor. Ginger also sensed that Judy lacked the conviction and belief that she could muster confidence and ownership of her need to get Ginger out of her personal space. Judy was at a disadvantage because Ginger was already in her space. Somehow, she had to move Ginger out. Most people attempt to continue to use the tools, but then they unconsciously step backward out of their personal space. As the client backs out of an area, the horse simply steps forward to follow them. This interesting dance of client backing up and horse moving forward into their space demonstrates a dance that we all do in our human relationships. People push in, so we back off to avoid conflict because we feel overpowered or not conscious of what is happening. Judy and Ginger looked like they were dancing. Ginger was the lead as she stepped forward, and Judy stepped backward.

I worked with Judy to develop a statement that would help her claim her authority and personal power and get young Ginger to stop crowding her. Ginger kept her precious doe-like eyes on Judy the entire time. Ginger looked thoughtful and intentional. Eventually, Judy came to the statement: "I deserve my space." I helped Judy bring that statement from her thinking mind down into her feeling body and lodge it below her stomach and belly button. This area in Chinese Qigong is the center of one's power and called the Dantian.

I then asked Judy to set her boundary again and ask Ginger to move out of her personal space. As Judy did so, Ginger continued to hold her ground and boldly stepped toward Judy yet again. Judy unconsciously stepped backward, acquiescing to Ginger's dominant behavior. Their dance continued, and Ginger was the leader, pushing very gently and persistently into Judy's personal space.

My coaching with Judy needed to go to the next level. I could see that she was on the verge of tears and starting to break down. Her "story" about her boundaries began to emerge. Before she went down the rabbit hole of her limitations, I had to catch her and shift her mind and consciousness instead into possibility and confidence. I guided her to use her body and brain to create a new reality. When this happens, things can feel tough for the client. They are about to break through old limiting perceptions. It is a very juicy moment and filled with potential at the same time.

Judy trusted my leadership, and she followed my lead. I told her that if I did not believe her, how could her horse? Ginger continued to stand and stare at her the entire time, not offering any gesture to move back out of Judy's space. I continued to coach Judy with statements such as "I can't feel the energy, Judy. Do you really mean it? Louder, Judy, declare your space, say your declaration from your belly. Own it, Judy, own what is yours."

Once again, Judy unconsciously took a small step back, and Ginger took a small step forward into Judy's space. Through more exploration, Judy's statement moved from "I deserve my space" to "I am worthy of being heard." I coached her again to own the statement. I encouraged her to voice it from her belly, coaxing her power with questions such as: "Do you want to be heard? I can't hear you; louder! What do *you* want? Do you deserve to be heard?" I asked her to place her hand on her Dantian and engage a new voice: "My voice matters. I matter." She then placed her left hand below her belly to ground her awareness of this center of power available to her. I coached her to stand her ground while continuing to use her new voice.

Then, the shift happened. I saw Judy's back lengthen with more strength. Her chest rose, and her shoulders came back. Her posture showed more confidence. Her new conviction came from her belly instead of her chest or throat. With every ounce of energy she had left inside her, she declared her right and worthiness to be heard. She claimed it with clear ownership and conviction and asked Ginger to back up one more time. Her statement and declaration rang true. At that moment, Judy was body-centered and congruent in her request. Suddenly, I could see a present, confident, and assured leader in the round pen. Ginger lifted a leg ever so slowly and gracefully and took one step back. Her soft eyes stayed on Judy. Judy burst into tears as she felt the surge of power moving through her body and the success of showing up in an entirely new and profound way.

I coached Judy again to say her statement with even more conviction. She waved the carrot stick and instructed Ginger to back out of her space. Ginger stepped back again and began to lick and chew, signs of energy moving, a newly established understanding, and a transparent communication exchange.

Judy, breathing deeply with tears falling down her face, declared her right to have her voice and be heard, no matter what others might want. She did not attempt to dominate Ginger. Judy achieved this feat not through her mind but through coming back into her body and using the life-force energy of her entire being to claim her needs and voice in relationship with another.

Later, Judy shared that although she wanted to play with Ginger, sentient beings need to understand and respect each other's space and limitations to play safely. Only then can the play be safe for both individuals. Judy revealed that in her family of origin, she was the peacemaker. She seldom asked of things from others and more often chose to go with the flow. She never wanted to make waves but instead focused on keeping others happy. Judy saw how this old conditioning kept her from claiming some of the deepest desires in her business and life. Outside, supported by nature, senses awake and alive, with another sensitive creature who knew how to test her conviction and strength, Judy reclaimed a lost part of her spirit, a more profound sense of her leadership. Judy moved away from the peacemaker role that she had become accustomed to earlier in life and began to speak up for what was most important to her.

There is no doubt that Judy had fewer issues expressing her needs and wants with people after the session. She had found her voice and the power to bring her entire being forward in engaging with another. She had claimed a part of herself that she had lost many years before. A few years after coming to this new understanding, Judy moved across continents and created an entirely new life.

REFLECTIONS

We all have times that we revert to our family of origin behaviors. We may become the rescuer, the martyr, or in Judy's case, the peacemaker. Each time we engage with these conditioned behaviors, we disregard part of our true nature, desires, and values. After years of living this way, we can become doormats, disengaged, or worse, depressed and despondent. But for Judy, a little horse named Ginger taught her how to find her voice to set boundaries and become the leader she was meant to be.

- When starting a new relationship, what sort of role do you unconsciously step into?
- How do you break free of old behavioral patterns?
- In new relationships, what part of your personal power needs to become more present?

Dancing with Horses

Horses live in herds in the wild. Because they are so vulnerable, they must live together to survive. That connection gives them purpose and meaning. If you spend time observing horse herd behavior, you will find they have dances that transpire in many forms. Stallions engage the dance of masculinity—seeking to conquer another stallion's mare. A young bachelor may have the dance of challenge with the herd's lead stallion. Two young bachelors jostle and play to release pent-up energy and gain muscle tone to eventually challenge the stallion. A stallion and mare may have a dance of courtship, seduction, and consummation, if the stallion is lucky. A mare and her foals have the dance of connection and disconnection, or need and freedom.

Just like our equine friends, we too need connection and to belong. In exploration of that need, we can feel highly vulnerable to the possibility of being hurt when our inner selves are revealed. Every time we interact with another there is a chance of this exposure, but embracing vulnerability is the birthplace of our strength. Shifting from a reactionary, surviving place to an internal environment allows us to take risks, reach out to others, and live our dreams.

Dancing with a horse might be something you have already imagined, a free-flowing connection with a horse that can be simultaneously heartwarming, grandiose, daring, or sensory-evoking. The horse as dancer may conjure within you archetypes such as the daredevil athletic agility of a circus performer, the grace evoked through a troupe of ballerinas, or the sensual and seductive energy of a couple exploring the passion of the tango. These images spark our hidden fantasies and an inner child or goddess that may never have been seen.

How can you hold the vision of "dance" and also ignite a fluid and synchronized contact with your horse? You must learn to let go of the need for perfection and stay with the desire to explore so you can experience deeper partnership, contact, fluid movement, connection, and harmony. The dance invites you to find the edges of space in communication with others and explore dynamic, unpredictable chemistry, deepening your ability to relate to others and self.

THE SACRED SPACE OF DANCE WITH HORSE

Dancing with a horse is a place of sacred space. You must enter into the ritual not through your head but through your heart and entire being. When you reach this open, non-judging state of being, the energy of a sacred space opens. At that moment, more than you could ever imagine can transpire with little effort, no ego, and no limits to the imagination. You become one in the journey.

This concept of "dance with horse" ignites me to the core of my being. The moments I've danced with my herd members have humbled me in a way that no other experience has. What I most want is for you to touch on this desire and courageously step forward to explore this concept for yourself. According to Wikipedia:

Dance is a performance art form consisting of purposefully selected sequences of human movement. This movement has aesthetic and symbolic value and is acknowledged as dance by performers and observers within a particular culture. Dance can be categorized and described by its choreography, its repertoire of movements, or its historical period or place of origin. An important distinction is to be drawn between the contexts of theatrical and participatory dance. Although these two categories are not always completely separate, both may serve special functions, whether social, ceremonial, competitive, erotic, martial, or sacred/liturgical.

There are numerous types of dance in every culture and society. Hip-hop, two-step, waltz, swing, and the cha-cha may be familiar to you. Whatever the form, dance reveals your vulnerability and your willingness to engage in a free-flowing connection.

As in all dances, there are "steps" to take when dancing with a horse, steps you might not have previously thought about or considered. These steps create a bond based on appreciation, reverence, and honor that will set the energy and intention for all other magnificent experiences to follow. However, the dancing I do with a horse has no "purposefully selected sequences of human movement." Instead, I enter into the field of the horse and ask the horse how he or she might like to move with me.

Dancing with a horse is happening every moment you are with your horse. The quality of that dance depends on you. Much of this quality comes from your ability to be present, reading, and receiving the communication your horse is offering. I let the horses call to me for the days they want to dance. I listen with my heart and follow their lead. When this happens, I set aside uninterrupted time to dance with my horses and treat it as a ritual or ceremony. The music selected comes intuitively—melding with the energy of the day, space, and my companion.

What I seek in these moments is engagement, acknowledgment of presence and flow, appreciation, and acceptance. When dancing with a horse, time slows down. I become one with a horse, and the wonder of what might be possible comes alive before my eyes, changing my life forever.

Sometimes I am gifted with a transcendence of reality and time. I am humbled, and I sink into great reverence and peace. Deep harmony moves through every cell of my body. I might feel as if the archetypal energy of the goddess, princess, maiden, circus performer, an innocent girl, or a queen is moving through me. Other times, it is rather lifeless or even frustrating, but even the frustrating times create a new level of understanding and connection with your horse. You must be willing to be vulnerable, to fall flat on your face, to let go of the ego so that you are not thinking about what others think. Your heart space must be open to always see what is possible and learn the horse's way of communicating. With this, you too can experience the heart dance with a horse you have always dreamed of having. Be willing to open yourself to the gift.

Dancing with a horse provides a way to explore fluid movement and connection with no set instructions or plan on what will transpire during the dance. When I am teaching someone this process, the participant selects the horse they want to dance with and the music that most resonates with them.

Typically, in these sessions, when a person is body-centered, free of agendas, and fully present to the moment, the horse, and the music, a flow transpires between horse and human. It is not about walking, trotting, or cantering transitions or any other training techniques. Dancing with a horse teaches you to understand how a horse responds to your energy, focus, the pressure of attention, and the quality of movements. Your horse also pays attention to what you are communicating through your breath. It is about a connection to yourself and developing a deeper relationship with your horse.

I had a private client, Julie, work with me for two days. In her last session, she decided she wanted to experience dancing with a horse. Julie and I worked together to prepare her for her session. She was versed in using the carrot stick. She had proven she was able to track her energy and emotions and also be sensitive to the body language the horse was offering her. She chose one of my favorite herd members.

Diva was a dirty, palomino-colored paint horse. Her coat was a stunning copper-penny color and her mane light blonde. She had black striping and spots on her legs, thus the word "dirty" in her coloring description. Diva was a very generous, willing, and giving mare. She had been a momma to five babies and was very laid back. Diva was the glue that kept my herd together, as she seldom, if ever, challenged anyone. She went with the flow and stayed out of the way of others. Many would say Diva was positioned lowest in the pecking order. However, when she left the ranch, all of the other horses had a complete meltdown and whinnied for at least thirty minutes, anxious that she might not return.

Julie stood outside the round pen area and first focused on becoming acutely aware of her energy and mood. She then kept her eyes on Diva and started to express all of the things she was appreciative of at the moment. As Julie did so, I noticed Diva lift her head from the blades of grass she was eating along the edge of the round pen. She turned her face and stared at Julie, and a connection began. Once Julie entered the round pen, Diva immediately left the short blades of grass. Both of them moved to the center of the round pen. Julie did some stretching as Diva stood quietly beside her.

Then Julie offered long gentle strokes along Diva's withers and her back. She whispered soft, tender, affirming statements as the early summer sun warmed both of their backs. As I watched, I noticed several species of birds suddenly showing up in the trees chirping lyrics I had not heard before. It was a very soft, quiet Sunday afternoon.

She asked Diva to go out to the edge of the round pen and Diva obliged. Then, the dance with Diva seemed a bit "sticky" or not flowing smoothly. Diva's body went from soft and relaxed to tense and watchful. Julie seemed less present in her body. Diva continued to get confused, and there was a lack of connection between the two of them. I asked Julie to stop the dance. We talked about what was happening to her. First, she realized that the music she picked was not working.

Next, I asked about what thoughts she was having while she was in her dance. She shared that she had thoughts based on doubt and worry. Caught in a nonproductive thought pattern, she wondered if Diva would dance with her, if she would look stupid, or if she might fail. I coached her back into her body awareness and back into the present moment. I reminded her of all the tools she could draw on that she had learned in our time together, to help her to stay centered on her being and free of limiting thought patterns. She focused on her heart space and returned to her words of appreciation and positive affirmations. Diva, watching intently from across the round pen, began to lick and chew.

We started the music again. This time, Julie and Diva moved around the round pen with ease and grace. Diva's lovely eye stayed focused on Julie as her body remained soft and flowing through several transitions, circling, coming in toward Julie, and moving back out to the rail. Julie moved with her. It was as if there was a string connected between them filled with a mystical tension that would not allow them to separate. The music she had selected was filled with sweet sorrow. At one point, my heart filled, and tears came to my eyes. She was allowing all of the pieces of her learning during the week (sorrow, letting go, becoming free, and owning her beauty) to move through her physical body. Diva was fully present with her, and they moved as partners.

From a distance, the dancing activity may look strange and seem very untraditional. Yet, what I see and experience with these sessions is that clients experience a pure, in the moment, artistic expression, shared with others without judgment.

As Julie moved and danced with the copper-penny-colored horse, Julie's inner beauty, even in sweet sorrow, radiated well beyond the round pen. She had come back home to her authentic expression while being connected to another in movement. Julie took the visceral experience of her horse dance back to her horses to build an even deeper relationship with them. It changed how they are on the ground together and in the saddle. Dancing with her horses deepens the relationship.

Julie also transferred this somatic learning to her everyday life, allowing more of her true essence to shine and be present in the world. If she leads herself into a positive, appreciative state of being, her connection with others will be much deeper than when she is in fear, doubt, and worry about others accepting her. She has a deeper understanding of how a doubt-filled mind stops the creative flow, and how following one's intuition and staying present in the moment creates ease.

The ability to be artful, to be spontaneous and creative is slowly diminishing in our culture. Technology keeps us focused on programs, functions, and predictable outcomes. So many people want a step-by-step guide to solving every situation in life that they are losing the ability to think creatively on their feet. Creative programs are diminishing, if not completely gone from our children's schools, robbing them of the ability to develop creative problem-solving skills and to experience a natural flow that happens when you are in your heart space and working in a nonlinear way. Horses appreciate this, as it is their way. They like to walk in curved lines; they meander, smell life, and have a timeless approach to the moments of the day.

I believe every person would benefit greatly from the art of dancing with a horse. The act helps you access your creative energy and childlike spontaneity. It challenges you to take chances, to let your true self out to play, shine, and be seen by others. It requires the engagement of the heart and the understanding of acceptance. It is living life as an art form. The world would be a different place with the level of open, heart-based flow in all of our relations that dance inspires.

REFLECTIONS

Consider the following steps before your own dance with a horse or immediately after:

- Who am I in this moment? (Take yourself through a quick body scan to identify your current mood and emotions.)
- What do I appreciate about myself, Mother Earth, and my horse at this time? What do I see and experience that touches my heart? (Acknowledge what is positive to bring positive energy forth.)
- Am I willing to explore the vulnerability of this relationship? (If your answer is yes to this question, you can proceed.)

- Center, breathe, and scan your body one more time.
- Open up the body through moving your arms, reaching for the sky, opening your chest area, twisting at your waist, and bending your knees a few times. Get all tension out of your body.
- Notice the environment. Tune into your sensory awareness, just like your horse does. Notice all of the sounds, how your skin feels, movement of air, quality of light and temperature, etc.

The Courting Period

The courting period is where you start to explore the relationship with your horse. You want to make a physical connection and say hello by scratching the withers, lightly rubbing the face, or with soothing strokes down the spine. As you offer these gestures, stay keenly aware of how your horse is responding—soft eyes or hardening, ears forward or pulling back, a slight movement of the head toward or away, body position shifting or changing, etc. Adjust and modulate your actions according to the response from the horse. Keep your heart open and take long, deep breaths to create presence.

You also want to explore the energy fields of your horse, the bubble of personal space, and how to use that field to create connection and disconnection. Again, notice many of the same signals—soft eyes or hardening, ears forward or pulling back, a slight move of the head toward or away, body position shifting or changing, etc. Adjust your closeness or distance as needed for the clear intention you are holding (pull toward or connect with). You may find that some horses are much more profoundly aware of this space than others. One of the benefits of the "dance" is that it helps the horse learn about their personal space if they previously lacked awareness from over-conditioning in early years of training.

Begin to Play and Explore

Allow yourself to explore in no particular order and with no real rules. Keep your eyes and heart on the horse and pay attention to how he or she responds to you. Do not try to play any role or archetype. Again, this is not about performance; it is about exploration. Ask yourself the following questions.

- What does the horse think is expected of them in a round pen area?
- Is my horse comfortable with the carrot stick?
- What does it mean for him/her?
- What draws this horse to me?
- What repels the horse?
- What creates curiosity?
- What brings the energy up?
- What brings it down?
- What are my partner's preferences?
- What happens when I breathe and smile?
- What happens when I get into my head?

Deepening into the Nuances of Fluid Contact

- What am I doing with my body?
- Where is my third chakra pointing?
- Put the lead line on your horse and explore your connection with your horse while using it.

- Share different positions and move with the lead line; notice how your horse responds.

- Explore where your horse is comfortable and flows.

- What is the quality of your balance? Are you secure in your core?

- Will he or she turn toward you if you step in front of the shoulder?

- When you step toward your horse, does he or she move away, remain unaffected, or look at you?

The above list outlines several components to experiencing a session of dancing with horses. I consider this type of engagement an advanced work. One must know horses at least at an intermediate level, and they must also have personal self-awareness, including their mood and emotions.

PART IV

Mustang Love—A Special Kind of Relationship

Hello, Wild Horse

One day I heard a voice in my head say, "What about the mustangs?" The nagging voice continued for months. I tried to let it go at first, but it got louder. "What about the mustangs?" I've heard this voice before; it is a clear neutral-toned voice and seems as if someone with more intelligence than myself is speaking to me. Often, when I follow an inner voice, new essential events, people, or animals come into my life.

Finally, with that in mind, I reached out to a woman named Ginger Kathrens. Ginger is a documentary videographer and advocate for the wild horses on our public lands. She is well known for her documentation of a wild stallion that lived in the Pryor Mountains of Montana named Cloud, the stallion of the Rockies. She followed him his entire life, recording his progress from birth to a stallion with his own herd. She created films demonstrating his interactions with other wild horses and stallions wanting to steal his mares, the dynamics of mustang families, and how they survive in the wild. She has recorded the family lineage of all of the Pryor Mountain horses and filmed them consistently for many years. This band of horses is unique, with their bloodlines and genetics traced back to the horses that the Spaniards originally brought with them from Europe. They are smaller in size and have short backs. They are highly intelligent because the herd has been wild for centuries with little to no new genetics introduced.

Ginger just happened to pick up the phone in her office when I called. She told me about a group of Pryor Mountain mustangs, gathered by the Bureau of Land Management, that were now in a holding facility in Colorado. The four horses were deemed untrainable and unrideable. Their destiny would be to live in a large, dry, dusty paddock with many other mustangs. They would be thrown hay at mealtimes and do a lot of nothing for the rest of their lives. It's basically a prison for horses and, ironically, is located within a state prison near Colorado Springs, Colorado.

As Ginger and I talked on the phone, she told me about the plight of the wild horses on our public lands and how she was an advocate for them. She began to speak about each of the four horses. At that moment, I felt an overwhelming presence and essence of a horse and saw the image of him in my mind's eye. With zero thought of future consequences, I heard myself say, "I'll take one." Little did I know what that choice would mean.

At that time, I was happily on my path as an author and teacher for the Equine Facilitated Learning and Coaching (EFLC) program. I had worked with many horses; in fact, my programs focus on connecting humans with their emotional intelligence and raising conscious awareness. I was comfortable with what I was teaching, and each day I was learning more and more horsemanship skills. However, those three little words changed my life forever.

A few months after that conversation, I found myself behind the walls of the Colorado prison. The day was cold, with just an inch or so of fresh snow on the ground. The skies were deep blue with puffy cottonball clouds, suggesting warmth that never arrived. It was spring in the Rockies. Ginger and I and two other women stood outside the gates until eventually, someone came to escort us through the property. We were driven in a truck past a large paddock that had hundreds of horses standing quietly in it. I was astonished to realize that many of those horses would never find a home or get beyond the walls that now contained their wild spirits and hearts. We slowly passed them and continued down the gravel road until we came to the main horse training area.

Within the prison was a "wild horse inmate program." The mustang I was to adopt was part of this program. The program creates opportunities for inmates to learn how to work with and begin the taming of wild horses that eventually become adopted by the public. Working with horses helps the inmates on their path of healing and learning new skills, while simultaneously training the wild horses and possibly finding homes for them. I found the entire process fascinating. I was in a world I knew nothing about, surrounded by many round pens, tons of horses, and inmates busily doing their jobs.

Because it was a correction center for men, every person in the equine training area was a man except for Ginger, one other woman, and myself. The inmate working with the horse that would eventually be mine seemed calm and gentle. I was wondering what turns he had taken in his life that had led him to this facility.

Unlike the younger, more trainable horses, the dark horse with brown around his nose that would eventually become mine was five and a half years old. His mind and instinctual understanding of the world was very developed and hardwired into his nervous system. He was a survivor and had lived in the mountains of Montana with lions, lightning storms, and long, snowy winters.

I had driven down from the mountains where I lived the night before. Rushing to get to my destination, I had only grabbed one jacket and failed to notice that it was bright blue and a bit slick. As I stood next to the five-year-old wild boy that day, I noticed that my coat was a bit noisy. So did he. He had great trepidation with me, and me with him.

He watched me intently as I reached up to stroke his withers. However, I noticed the muscles of his body stiffened. It was not the joyful first meeting I had envisioned. The other three women with me were all having a different experience. None of the horses seemed all that excited about the humans around them. One pulled back from the bar he was tied to, resisting the rope so strongly I feared he would hurt himself. Another reared and fussed, then came down on all fours and began to run around.

That horse was going to the most experienced horsewoman in the group, which was clearly not me. My body experienced so many mixed emotions and moods of those around me, and it evoked in me a profound heaviness. All of the inmates had worked with one horse only. Each one had achieved different levels of success with his horse. By the time we left, I felt tired and sad to know that I would be taking the inmate's friend away. Would it break the inmate's heart?

The agreements became concrete as I signed the paperwork. Ginger and the rest of our group left the facility. I climbed in my car, and as I drove the winding mountainous road home, a mixture of excitement and anticipation began to build inside of me. I daydreamed about what would happen when my new horse arrived at the ranch. I fantasized about riding my new, wild horse. We would go from Mexico to Wyoming and bring attention to the plight of the wild horses. I envisioned us traveling cross-country, offering demonstrations to continue the awareness.

In all of my fantasies, I was an amazing cowgirl, riding my steadfast stead off into the sunset—with the awe of everyone around me, of course. Two wild and free spirits partnered, and at some level, helping all wild horses. I felt called to this mission, a perfect combination of adventure and purpose. Little could I know, this Spanish mustang would take me on another journey, far from my ego-based fantasies.

I named him Corazon de la Montana, Heart of the Mountain. His nickname is Cor, which means "theft" in Arabic and "love" in French. (I tell my clients, "He will steal your heart.") The program inmates had trained him for the halter, worked with his hooves, and put a saddle on him, intending to teach Corazon how to be a domesticated horse in a human world.

I was relatively new to domesticated horses when the little wild horse I named Corazon arrived at the ranch. Domesticated horses are conditioned by repetitive training to conform to the desires and wishes of the humans who handle them. Most domesticated horses, if appropriately trained and treated well, will go on to live a life serving humanity. These horses are typically agreeable and appease human desires. The wild mustang in front of me was a completely different animal. This highly sensitive horse was hardwired to react to anything that might be dangerous or threaten his well-being. His primary mode in life was to survive. His instincts were finely tuned. I had no idea how to handle him. When the man who delivered him to the ranch arrived, he asked me, "Shall I take the halter off?" In my ignorance, I said, "Sure." Additionally, the only place to put him was in a round pen.

One month later, I was still trying to catch him. Cor relentlessly fought for his freedom—I could not even touch him. He was scared of me, and I was terrified of him. He was fast, reactive, and when not in motion, he would stare into the distant hills, longing for his freedom and family in Montana. As I watched him process these dramatic life changes, my emotions ran the gamut from pity, regret, and complete self-doubt, to fear and deep sadness.

I did all of the soft-building relationship skills. I would sit for hours on the other side of the metal bars, reading, and sharing time. He showed absolutely zero interest in me. I would try to feed him grass with my hand through the fence. He would look at me, put his little nose down as if to take some, then bolt to the other side of the round pen. If I entered the round pen, he would stay on whatever edge was farthest from me. I had no skills to work with him, catch him, and put a halter on him. He claimed every moment of freedom he could during every single one of my attempts to make friends.

Eventually, I called a very experienced horsewoman, Jaime, whom I had met when I went to see Corazon behind the prison walls. Her wild horse had already jumped an eight-foot fence and tried to mate with one of her horses. Because this group of horses was older, all of them had stallion-like tendencies. I knew nothing about working with stallions. (However, after eleven years with Corazon, I am now very well versed in stallion behavior and can easily predict what will set him off.)

Jaime and I worked with Corazon (well, Jaime mostly did, for a full day). We had both agreed that we would not run him endlessly around the pen. He was fit as a fiddle and after living in the mountains wild and free his entire life, could effortlessly go all day in circles. Instead, we decided it needed to be his choice. Day one passed, and we went home at 8:00 p.m. We had made little advancement. A month without a halter on with no human interaction had only allowed for him to return to his known wild ways.

The next day we got more of the same. She and I would take turns, and she would give me tips on how to understand his movement and influence him. Luckily, Jaime is not an arrogant trainer. She was also willing to listen to my ideas and thoughts. At noon, I suggested that we get creative and bring in additional panels to shrink the extra-large permanent round pen. She loved the idea. We held fast to our agreement that we would not force Corazon. He had to offer himself and offer to put his head into the halter. The round pen kept getting smaller, and he kept going in circles.

Near the end, the continually modified round pen ended up being less than about eight feet in diameter. Corazon continued to play his little tricks of walking around, scouting out, and his eye was on Jaime more than ever. Slowly he started to give the signs he was ready.

His head lowered during his walk. He began to sniff the ground, and he would turn his entire head and look at her. Then suddenly, he stopped. He looked at me, and he looked at her. Then, he approached Jaime and stood beside her. He allowed her to stroke his withers and then, eventually, he dropped his head into the light rope halter. It was one of many big sighs of relief to come during my relationship with this wild horse.

We moved him into his new smaller paddock area, and I spent the next few weeks getting him accustomed to me putting a halter on him. I let him smell me, and he allowed me to touch him. I would walk him around the ranch so he could see what it was all about. It took me months to realize that some of the fear that I felt every time we were together was not all mine. My highly empathic nature was picking up on his trepidation and fear. The intensity of the journey I had embarked upon became crystal clear at that moment. He was going to teach me how to be a better leader. Not just in my skills, but also my ability to be emotionally agile and secure for him. My relationship with him has been the hardest of my life, but the most rewarding on a multitude of levels.

REFLECTIONS

While life events can be challenging, they can also provide many gifts. My choice to adopt Corazon was beyond my wildest dreams in so many ways, both demanding and rewarding. Those moments are what help us expand, learn, and change our lives.

- When have you listened to the clear voice in your head only to find yourself being stretched in many ways?
- When did you last act on a deep internal calling?
- What might it be like to allow yourself to step into great unknowns and have the ride of your life?
- Do you tend to stay small and doubt yourself? If so, what might be possible if you grabbed the reins and truly lived life to the fullest?

Really, Again?

Aworld-renowned horse trainer came to a barn where I once boarded my wild mustang, Corazon. The clinician was an easy-mannered man with a quiet demeanor. Lost on how I could accomplish successfully saddling Corazon, and still with no trainer to work with me, I asked the man for some help. He came to meet my horse.

The trainer proceeded to work with Cor in the round pen. I watched as he moved my horse in one direction and then the next. Cor had his eye on him, and with every move that he made, there was a conversation happening between the two of them. They seemed to reach a level of understanding—it was impressive. Then it came time to put the saddle on. As soon as the tall, calm man went to the fence and grabbed the saddle, Corazon's body stiffened, and his eyes became glued to the saddle. Cor wanted nothing to do with the heavy leather item.

The trainer approached Cor, and Cor scooted away. Corazon continued to say, "No." The skies shifted as heavy gray clouds moved in. The temperature dropped, and it started to sprinkle. Then, I noticed the demeanor of the trainer changed. He had shifted out of a very relaxed state, and his body muscles became firmer and his mood more determined. He told me he wanted to hobble my horse, which is essentially tying his two front legs together so that his ability to run would be severely limited. He let me know that he had done this many times. I felt my body instantly constrict in resistance to the idea, but since the trainer was high level, who was I to challenge him? I handed over my power and allowed him to do what I knew, deep down in the core of my being, was not the right thing.

The saddle had now been placed back up on the rail, far away from Corazon. Corazon stood still and watched the trainer. Then, the trainer knelt and tied his legs with a rope. It was a makeshift hobble system. Cor stared straight at me, his eyes penetrating every cell of my body. The light rain continued as the sky shifted from gray to dark gray hedging on black. The air felt thick with moisture, and the sprinkles continued to fall. Corazon continued to stand completely still. Once the trainer had the hobbles in place, he once again attempted to place the heavy western saddle on Cor's back. Cor bucked and bolted, reared, and danced. The round pen became a dust bowl, and I feared for my horse's safety. The saddle went flying, and eventually, the hobbles broke free from Corazon's hooves. No surprise, I felt relief. Corazon was one sturdy and opinionated little black horse.

The trainer then shifted into a more dominant position as his desire to achieve this goal became more intense. He moved briskly and with determination. Corazon stood still in one spot. The sprinkles turned to raindrops and I felt the temperature drop even further. Once again, the trainer fastened the ropes around my horse's legs, and once again, Corazon stared at me. I felt his entire being penetrating my consciousness as I heard him say, "Really, again? Do you need to see this again? Okay." I did not know what to do. I could not find my voice to stop the trainer. I knew the same result would be forthcoming. Corazon just kept staring at me.

Once the clinician tightened the saddle strap, Cor began bucking, kicking, and dancing until the ropes came off again. He had moved halfway around the circular pen and now was only a few feet away from me. The rain was now coming steadily down, and the trainer was slipping around as the ground became muddy. Cor stood there, shaking and staring at me with the ropes loose around his feet. With all the personal power I could muster, my squeaky voice asked the six-foot, well-respected trainer if we could stop. He agreed reluctantly because of the rain. He let me know he would be happy to try again the next day.

I took Cor back to his paddock, and that was the first time I apologized to my horse. I apologized for my lack of personal power to stop the trainer. I apologized for not standing up for the truth I knew inside myself. I apologized for allowing this to happen to him. He stared at me blankly through it all, and then simply walked away. I spent that night beating myself up and doubting my ability and worth to have this horse in my life.

I did not have the trainer work with him again. I had no judgment of the trainer. Corazon is a unique horse and knows who he is to his core. He had challenged every trainer who worked with him. He would continue to fight for any freedom he still had. I continued with Cor the best I could. We would take one step forward, and I would be ecstatic. Then, often, we would take two steps back. I wish I could say I was above all of those dominant, ego-driven approaches, but I can't.

A few weeks later, I wanted to take Cor to a friend's place to see some new things and practice in her obstacle course. He refused to load. I continued to ask the same way, with the same approach, and I got the same answer. Frustration boiled in my belly, and my anger rose. My techniques digressed into attempts of complete dominance. Every time I asked him to load, he would simply stand still and stare at me—his strong presence and high confidence persisting beyond my own.

I became so angry that I lashed out and struck him with my training stick. At first, he pulled back in shock; I had never done that before. Then, he planted his four hooves and stood there. I heard him say, "Go ahead. You can't touch my spirit with that stick." I whacked him once more, and with his solid, unflinching stance, the shame of my actions moved through me like a hot burning wave. I dropped to my knees and sobbed.

He continued to stand solid while glaring at me, purposely showing me my dark side of attachment and dominance. I hated myself at that moment. I hated that I could not figure out how to be a friend or a good leader for my horse. I felt that I was wrong and worthless. That shame was followed by helplessness because nothing I did mattered. Then, I did what everyone tells you not to do, and I simply gave up. With my shoulders heavy and my mind clouded by self-judgment, I walked with Corazon back to his stall. He walked through the gate, never looked back, and went to the pile of hay leftover from earlier. Corazon had revealed the dark, angry, shadow side of my personality. No longer could I think I was superior or righteous.

As painful as that moment was, ultimately, it set me free emotionally. I began to look more deeply at my own shadow side. I learned to accept myself and the power of anger, and as I did so, it controlled me less. Months went by, and I continued to try everything I knew how to do with Corazon. We progressed some, but I still did not have the skills I felt I needed to understand this proud, independent, and unrelenting horse. Eventually, we found someone who helped us tremendously. Corazon began to accept his new life, and I began to understand his needs. About six months later, I had my first ride on my proud mustang by the name of Corazon de la Montana (Heart of the Mountain).

REFLECTIONS

Allowing our unconscious agendas to take over is easy. We can push beyond what is appropriate and lose touch with how our actions may be affecting another. This can lead to dangerous situations we then regret.

- If you have the responsibility of another, how many times do they need to show or tell you what they need before you respect it?
- Where do you see ego-based choices bring up resistance in your horse?
- How can you shift your energy to be more conscious?
- What can you do to build or regain trust?
- What dark side of your personality do you try to hide? What might be possible if you allowed yourself to be humbled by a horse and heal those emotions?

Don't Put Me Down

Spring was in the air, the grass was green, and the horses were happy to be grazing. I had moved my mustang, Corazon, to the ranch where my trainer Doug lived. Doug had helped us tremendously and it was time for Corazon and me to go deeper in our relationship, and I was keen to start riding him.

At the new ranch, Doug was riding him up to four times a week. Corazon had started to come along nicely. He was very agreeable, once he had a clear understanding that the saddle on his back and the rider who then sat in it were not out to kill him, like a predator in the wild mountains of Montana. He had taken a long time to understand that although humans are predators that stalk and have very focused intentions, we do not kill and eat horses like the lions in the wild lands to the north.

Corazon had been staying in a paddock he shared with another mustang. The two of them were in the center of the five hundred-plus acre equine boarding facility. Snowcapped peaks, crystal clear blue skies, and streams running with fresh snow water at least provided a somewhat wilderness feel compared to the previous boarding facility where I had placed him. Additionally, there were over one hundred head of horses at this location. Corazon was pleased to be in the middle of all of the action.

We had several days in a row of success with Corazon. He was listening more intently, and the level of pushback and resistance to all of the human tools and strappings had significantly diminished. Doug announced that he was heading out of town, and he planned to place Corazon in the big pasture with all of the other horses. I was heading to Belgium for two weeks to teach.

With Corazon moving into a new herd, and with the trainer and I both being away, I immediately found myself in high resistance and saying "No." I explained that I felt we could not make that dramatic of a change to Corazon's environment. I had two fears. First, the ranch was not willing to put him out for a few hours at a time so Corazon would go from eating harvested dry grass onto pasture—full time. Second, I feared it would confuse him. My gut said that Corazon would worry he had been cast aside and abandoned. The trainer laughed at me and said I was way too sensitive. At that moment, I even doubted my knee-jerk gut reaction. Why would he not like being put out to pasture? The terrain was rolling hills with a large herd of horses. It would be the closest thing to wild Corazon would experience since being captured over a year ago. The trainer reminded me that he was a wild horse and that he used to survive on his own. I stated my objections again, but they went unheard. The next day, Corazon was moved to the more extensive, hilly pasture, and Doug left for his trip.

I was busy preparing for my trip that was just days away. I had also gotten caught up in being an advocate for the wild horses. A new law was going to pass in the Senate, possibly, and I was busily focused on gathering signatures on a petition to prevent it. Two days passed, and I had not seen my horse. I had been spending every day with him and knew I had to get up to the ranch. I dropped everything and drove to the farm. As I drove to the pasture, I could see the herd up on the hillside. Everyone was grazing happily among the sagebrush and wildflowers. However, I could not see Corazon.

Once I arrived at the ranch, I walked out to the large gate next to an old cement watering hole. There I found my little black horse lying down. Immediately, I knew that something was wrong. I looked in the watering hole and saw a dead bird floating around. Damn. I put his halter on him and proceeded to talk to him. He slowly got up. I led him over to rich, thick green grass. He dropped his head and barely attempted to nibble. Then he dropped down onto the ground and began to roll back and forth. He placed his belly on the ground and rubbed it hard. My heart sunk. Even without much horse experience, I knew this was not a good sign.

I walked him back to the barn and asked the assistant manager of the facility if she had noticed anything off about him. She said she had seen him lying by the watering hole for two days. I have no idea why she did not call me about his behavior. To say I was pissed is an understatement. What unfolded through the next forty-eight hours was one of the toughest situations I have had with him. I once again found myself in a situation with minimal experience or knowledge, and Corazon faced something that I believed he could not fight alone: colic. Colic is when the small or large intestines of a horse cannot process the food properly, and there is an obstruction or a twist that prevents movement through the passage. It can kill a horse.

The vet arrived in a few hours, and we proceeded to do all we could for Corazon, hoping that his demeanor would change, he would eliminate (letting us know his digestive system was working again), and start eating. The vet put a long tube down his throat and poured mineral oil through the tube so that it would act as a laxative, moving the waste from his body. It did not work. The vet suggested I haul him to the clinic for observation through the night. I was reticent to move him yet again, into a completely new environment, and especially into a small cement stall that resembled a prison cell. The vet left.

Three hours later, we were hauling him down to the facility. Once there, they were able to stabilize him and the vet told me to go home. Someone would be on call all night. They would call me immediately if something came up. By then, I was exhausted, dehydrated, feeling hungry, entirely overwhelmed, scared out of my mind, and filled with anxiety. I could only imagine how my horse was feeling. I paced the floors of my house for hours until I made myself lay down. It did not feel right to me. I fell asleep, and within two hours, I woke. A peaceful calm moved through my body, and instinctively, I knew he was doing better. I took a big sigh of relief and fell back to sleep.

About 4:30 a.m., I woke again. I bolted up to a seated position and instantly knew something was off. Pacing back and forth, thoughts of worry, fear, and doubt consumed my mind. *What was happening to Corazon? How could I find out? What were they doing with him?* The office said they would call me if something happened, and they had not; maybe I was just neurotic. Unable to wait any longer, I called the office. No answer. I left a message saying I sensed something was wrong, and I needed a call back as soon as possible. They called me at 6:00 a.m. to tell me there were complications in the early hours of the morning, and they were doing all that they could for him.

I rushed to the office, only to find my horse in a metal contraption completely tight around his body so he could not rear, buck, or even move. Corazon stood perfectly still, muscles tense, and drenched with sweat. His eyes were bulging out of their sockets. The whites were showing the level of fear he was experiencing. He stared at me with an anxious silent plea for me to help him. Meanwhile, the vet and his young technical protégées scurried around him and injected him with medicines and inserted long needles to suck blood for testing. I was horrified and felt helpless. What was happening? It felt off, but I had no experience in what was happening. Corazon looked like a science project. The room filled with adrenaline between Corazon, the vet, his protégées, and me.

The vet told me he had started to pace and stir in the small, tight stall where they had placed him for the night. And, even though Corazon had released some manure, the vet's advisement was dismal—either do surgery or put him down. Surgery was expensive, and many horses do not survive through it. He also wanted me to know that a lot of his clients wanted to do an autopsy after the horse was put down so they could better understand what had happened. He thought it might help me to know why it had been necessary. Then he said he would be happy to pay for that process since this was his first wild horse, and he was interested to know what was going on. All sorts of red flags went up. Yet, being the highly sensitive person I am, I do not always think clearly under pressure. I told him to put Corazon back into the stall and to give me a bit of time to decide what to do. He pressured me a bit, letting me know I did not have a lot of time, and that it was unfair to the horse.

I called several friends to help me process the decision and finally went with my gut. I told the vet, "no." I said that if this little wild horse were going to die, he would die breathing fresh air, laying in green grass, and with the blue sky above him. A friend, Susan, arrived a few hours later, and she applied an old massage technique she learned from a rancher where she had grown up in Wyoming. The method helps to clear the cecum area of the intestine located between the small and large intestines. This area can be sensitive to sudden shifts in a diet (he had been put out into a field after living in a paddock for months) or bacteria (he was drinking from a water source with a dead bird floating in it) and can contribute to a colic situation. We stood next to Corazon, and she talked me through the process. Corazon was not interested in the way I applied the technique. My energy was on edge with fear for his future. He was side-stepping away from me. I asked her to try. He then shifted his entire hind end toward us. Susan was well known as a calm, big-hearted horse person, and loved by many people. She had also raised and trained many foals. She massaged him gently.

Thirty minutes later, he released a small pile of manure. My vet still insisted that he did not think he would make it. The ranch manager approved me bringing him home, even if he were to arrive and then die. Susan left to fetch her trailer. The vet marched off angrily.

Two hours later, we walked Corazon out of this small cement stall, and Susan opened the trailer door. Simultaneously, another trailer pulled up, and a horse was unloaded. The vet walked over, said a few words to the person who brought the horse, and then injected the horse. The horse dropped dead to the ground with a loud, heavy, ominous thud. Corazon watched intently. He has never liked getting into trailers. I am sure it is from the trauma of being rounded up and forced into metal pens and horse trailers, and then hauled away to the strange world of humans. However, it was a different story on this day. Immediately after hearing the loud thump as the horse dropped to the ground, Corazon walked toward Susan's trailer. I followed, he jumped in, we shut the door, and we all got the heck out of there.

When we pulled into the ranch, all one hundred horses that occupied it began to cry and neigh in acknowledgment of his return. A herd gathered and ran along with the trailer as we moved down the driveway. Tears swelled in my eyes as I said a prayer inside, asking for good health as I knew we were not fully out of the woods yet.

That night, I could not leave him. I laid next to his stall listening to every movement and sound he made. When the soft light of dawn came, I knew the storm had passed. It had been forty-eight hours of confusion, shifting, pain, fear, and finally relief. Clearly, it was not Corazon's time to go down.

REFLECTIONS

My interactions with Corazon have taught me so much about trust, sensitivity, and perception. There is the trust between us, and there is the trust within me to follow my intuition and do the right thing, even if it isn't the obvious thing to do. When I follow my instinct, the outcome is always good; when I lack the trust to follow my senses, the outcome becomes precarious.

- When have you listened to your intuition, and made a different choice against the advice of others, that turned out to be the right one?
- In stressful situations, do you turn inward or outward for answers?
- What do you trust more, your gut or someone else's perspective?
- How can you be more aware of what your instinct is telling you?

Broken Trust Mended

There is a chance in every relationship that trust might be broken. The question is, can it be repaired and eventually create an even deeper level of connection and bond, or does the relationship completely break down and the parties involved go their separate ways? Corazon de la Montana continues to teach me about the importance of trust in a relationship. His wild ways and highly tuned instincts examine my motives and my levels of leadership every day. I am convinced that he knows me better than I know myself.

Corazon has done well with his transition from the wild mountains of Montana to the human world. During our first year together, we spent an enormous amount of time bonding, sometimes through doing nothing, other times during training, introducing him to new things, or his favorite time: when he gets to eat. He trusts me and, therefore, other humans. Unfortunately, it only takes one human doing the wrong thing that can break the trust we have built. And everything digresses.

Horses receive their vaccinations in the spring. One vaccination, for the strangles virus, requires a skinny straw to be placed inside the horse's nostrils, and then the vaccination is sprayed up their nose. As you can imagine, not too many horses enjoy this. When the vet came to give spring shots, I was busy with a program and could not be present. I did not even think to suggest that Corazon not receive the strangles vaccination. Instead,

I completely trusted my veterinarian's judgment and methodology for administering the vaccination. After all, I had seen him work with Corazon before, and Corazon seemed completely comfortable with this man.

Unfortunately, I discovered later that it was the vet tech who administered the vaccination. She befriended Corazon, stuck the straw up his nose, shot the fluids in, then stepped backward with relief and an exclamation, "I did it!" At the same time downright startling Corazon. He was not so sure what had just crept up on him and what the heck was happening to his nose. He was not happy, to say the least.

I went to visit Corazon the next day. I approached him in the usual way, not knowing what had happened. He wanted nothing to do with me. Around and around the pasture we went. At times I could get near him, but as soon as I reached to touch his neck, he would take off running. At the time, I concluded that it was because I had not been out to see him for over a week. Plus, there was a cold wind blowing in from the north, making all the horses rambunctious.

The next day, I brought Corazon from the pasture, and my trainer Doug and I worked with him. We both noticed how different he was acting. His attention was not entirely with me, as his head was slightly cocked away from me. He was reticent to allow my hands around his head and nose. He seemed more sensitive than he had in months. It seemed that we had taken not only one step backward but two. I focused on some basic foundational processes in the round pen. I asked him to join up, follow along, turn in, and transition, all to build connection and communication with him. Both Doug and I were mystified. What had happened to Cor that he wanted so little to do with us?

The next day, Doug connected the dots. He told me how Corazon had reacted strongly when the vet had administered the spring vaccinations.

At the time, Doug did not think much of it. They had over fifty head of horses to get to, and time was of the essence. He admitted that what had happened during the vaccination had indeed broken trust with Corazon. Corazon had experienced a human sneaking up on him and tricking him, then directly after that, having discomfort and pain in his nostrils. In a wild horse's mind, that is betrayal. We headed back to the round pen, where we worked to rebuild the relationship with Corazon and minimize his concerns about being touched around the head and especially his nose.

Doug and I spent several sessions working through the broken trust between Corazon and humans. A wild horse, especially one that has lived in the wild for over five years, does not just go back to what is expected of him. He is hardwired only to engage when he feels safe and only with those who are trustworthy. Eventually, Corazon came around. Now, he trusts both of us again, and to some degree, I believe he trusts us even more. We knew and accepted that his behavior and desire to disconnect was a form of communication; he was not misbehaving. He was letting us know that the relationship was no longer the same. We were also willing to invest the time needed to rebuild trust (we had the patience to stay in the conversation with him). Because we had already built a strong foundation of trust with Corazon, we were able to reestablish that trust versus starting from scratch with no form of trust at all. Still, it was not a quick process.

Trust is not a simple thing. Nor is it permanent. It has many nuances around intention, honesty, kindness, straight talk, consistency, reliability, and the level of one's abilities and skills. Horses in the wild extend trust as needed to form relationships, belong to a band (wild herd), procreate and build their own family, and have a higher chance of surviving. Wild horses are always on the lookout for what might eat them, what might harm them, and who has ill intentions. Without this highly developed capacity, they may find themselves as a dinner for a lion. They depend on each other's ability to identify danger so that they can flee and find safety. Horses need to depend on each other, and a single horse cannot survive in the wild. There will be no one to look over him as he sleeps and no one to share the responsibility of finding water and food and to maintain safety. Horses follow and extend the most significant level of trust to those who demonstrate a higher level of trustworthiness.

In my human-to-human relationships, I have ended relationships because of broken promises, betrayal, and hurt that I felt could not be restored. I have stepped away from budding relationships because of gut feelings that the person was not trustworthy. Human-to-human relationships can be just as complicated because each individual will have different needs with trust. I have also welcomed people back into my life after they have broken trust. I chose to mend and repair the relationship because I could feel the other person's good intentions. In these times, I had to find my place of heart-based power, a situation of knowing that I would be okay no matter what the circumstance around me. Each time of extended trust or distrust was a learning lesson for me.

As I work with Corazon, he deepens my understanding of how trust wilts, buds, and eventually can bloom again. These cycles can only happen through the nurturing of each being in the relationship. Both parties must have the willingness and commitment to understand before judging and to have patience and courage to explore what is possible. One must ask what caused the breakdown of trust, and does each party know how it affects the individual? One must be prepared to say they behaved poorly or lacked having the other's physical or emotional needs in mind. To mend broken trust, we must be willing to pause, take inventory, address the wrong, and make it right. It is an investment of the heart and of time. One must be ready to be humble. As Corazon steps into another level of accepting the human world and me, it sparks me to become a better person for him. His trust in me has inspired me to extend the same to him. To be in a relationship with him, I must be willing to grow.

REFLECTIONS

Life can move quickly. When we have things to get done it is easy to miss important communications from others and trespass on their sensitivities, sometimes without realizing what happened. Corazon is sure of who he is, and of what is safe. While slow to trust, when he does, it is based on respect and acknowledgment of a true partnership. He is not quick to forgive but eventually, with slow, clear steps, he is willing to allow the trust to return.

- If someone has broken trust with you, how do you react?
- If you break trust with another and then want to reestablish the relationship, what steps would you need to take?
- When have you judged another's behavior instead of realizing they are simply communicating something to you? What might be possible if you saw all behaviors as a form of communication?

Metal Boxes

There are a lot of ways to be with horses and a lot of ways to train horses. If there is one horse in my life who has taught me this lesson, it would be Corazon de la Montana. He was a wild stallion until he was five and a half years old before he came into the human world, but not by choice. Imagine what it would be like to be a wild horse on public lands, grazing in harmony with your broader or larger herd, enjoying nature with your hooves solidly on the ground, and embracing all of the changes in the weather and the rhythm of nature.

Corazon was originally named "Grizzly" by Ginger Kathrens of the Cloud Foundation, who photographed and filmed him in Montana. She goes to Montana regularly to film this special herd of Pryor Mountain mustangs. The horses' bloodlines trace back to the Spanish Barb horses brought over by the Spanish Conquistadors during the days of colonization. The Spanish Barb horses are smaller, have short backs, and are quite muscular. They are brave, powerful, and kind horses. Ginger travels the long trek from Colorado Springs up to Lowell, Montana, to visit the wild herd. She has documented their lives and has tracked the genealogy of all of the different families. She is an advocate for their freedom and has witnessed hundreds of wild horses being removed from the public lands.

Imagine that you are on the mountainside, and you are in peace, standing in a field filled with lupines, buttercups, daisies, and blanket flowers.

You are grazing through the green, lush fields before the late summer sun pulls all of the moisture from the plants, and everything turns to a golden, dry hue. Imagine that the air is cool and the birds are chirping and you are in great harmony on the land with plenty to consume.

Then, imagine that from out of nowhere, and quite unexpectedly, a helicopter flies up over a ridge, something you've never seen before; a large bird of sorts, with huge propellers whisking through the air. It's a frightening visual, with the sound of thunder and chaos. Without thought, the instinct of the whole herd surrounding you is to run as fast as they can to get away from the monster in the sky. And that is exactly what you do too. You follow with your herd, charging down the mountainside with the helicopter looming above you, moving from one side to the other to influence and control the direction that you and the herd take. Heavy breathing and the pounding of your hooves on the earth feeds your body with more and more adrenaline, consuming your every cell. The only thing you can focus on is staying close and tight with your herd, going as fast as you can, and making sure you don't fall.

Finally, up ahead you see all of these strange, large, square, metal containers with people waving white flags above their heads lining metal fencing. The adrenaline is so high that all the herd knows to do is to go directly into this area. Surrounded now by metal fences, there's clanging and banging and all of your family members and you are completely frightened. Your natural response to flight has now been taken away from you, and fear fills every cell of your body, consuming you. Without the flight response, you are lost. Some of your herd members begin to fight, kicking out and trying to jump the fences. Others go to a corner while others are still running around, releasing adrenaline through the flight response. Then, the men with the white flags start waving you all down an even more narrow area of fencing. As you and your mates panic, hooves hit the fence, men yell, dust is flying; everybody is in a panic. You have an unknown future ahead, not knowing where you are going but being forced to move into an even tighter area.

As this metal fencing narrows, one of your friends falls and the others can't help but stampede over that body, taking his life. High adrenaline and deep fear is pulsating through every equine being. Once down that chute, all of a sudden you are forced up a metal ramp and into a large metal box. Hooves hit metal floors covered with rubber for the first time in your life, not understanding the texture and sound or the feeling of the floor. It's not safe. It's all foreign. Metal walls with small windows surround you. You're crammed in with all of your friends. Everybody is shaking with fear. Eyes are white. Everyone is covered with sweat and dust. No one knows what is happening.

Before you know it, the last wall of the metal box is shut, taking the day's light with it. Now you are inside of a horse trailer. Hooves are hitting the sides of the walls, chains are rattling, and all of a sudden, the box begins to move. What you don't realize in this moment is that you will never return to the life you knew.

I think it is ridiculous that any human being who adopts a wild horse thinks the horse is going to have an easy time adapting to their new world. It is folly to think that after such trauma to their physical, mental, emotional, and spiritual being, they would easily conform to another's desires or wishes. Yet, many people objectify the horse and reduce it to a thing to control versus a being to understand and commune with. The comprehension of the depth of the wildness in some of these horses cannot really be understood until you live with one on a day-to-day basis.

I share this concept and invite you to embrace what it would be like to be a wild horse brought in from wild lands so that you could then understand what it would be like to be a wild horse in captivity. You have lost your home, you are no longer free to run on mountain ridges. Instead, you are forced to step into metal boxes and be transported to places unknown.

Unfortunately for me, I did not have a lot of experience loading horses into trailers before Corazon de la Montana came into my life. With all of the different trainers who helped me, never once did the loading of this horse go easily. It took approximately eight years for Corazon to be able to keep his mind and stay present, and not go into a trauma response when loading into a trailer.

There were more situations than his capture that fed Corazon's reluctance to be in a trailer. One afternoon, I decided to load him up and take him to a ranch near Aspen, Colorado, where I was boarding another of my horses that he was friends with. My boyfriend's daughter was going to start riding Corazon. I was still not a good enough rider to ride him regularly, and she needed a project. She was a brave fourteen-year-old; it was a perfect match. On this particular day, I was taking Corazon back to the ranch where he stayed most of the time. A ranch hand had offered to help load Corazon. I gave explicit instructions to the ranch hand to never shut the back gate of the trailer until I told him to do so. I let him know that Corazon and I would probably come out of the trailer a couple of times and that I would only shut that door when I felt Corazon was ready to be in the trailer. My way of working with Corazon was to give him a lot of choice in the process.

The ranch hand said, "Yeah, yeah, yeah, I know how to do this." I wish I'd paid more attention to his attitude. I asked only three times before

Corazon jumped into the trailer. Before I knew it, the ranch hand began to shut the door. Corazon began to step out of the trailer. Right before my eyes, I saw Corazon's leg get pinched between the trailer and the gate swiftly shutting. This only caused a bigger response from Corazon, pulling and backing out and pushing against the gate. My ranch hand had no choice but to open it and out my horse went, blood dripping all over the ground. Corazon had cut his lower leg.

Great, I thought. Not only did this man not listen to me and respect where I'd gotten with this horse, but he also allowed his ego to get in the way and override my instructions. The cost was to my horse. Now, Corazon had been "bit" by the predator, the trailer. The trailer was now a big lion, something evil. In the wild, if he cut his lower leg like that, it could mean death for him. If he cut himself on any of his lower extremities, it could cause him many problems and lead to fatality.

After that day, loading Corazon in the trailer became more and more problematic. And, frankly, it was *that* trailer. I could load him in larger trailers if I put one of my other horses in first; he would jump right in and go. But when I tried putting him in the smaller trailer by himself, or even with another horse, he would be reticent. Because he knew that *this* trailer is the one that caused him pain.

So, I had a wild horse, a strong-headed, intelligent, willful horse that often and always asked, "Why am I doing this? What is the purpose? Is it going to bite me again?" He was never one to just do something for the sake of doing it unless it brought him joy, which I learned later.

Once I arrived at the small ranch where I currently live, I let go of all the training of Corazon. I had ridden him several times, others had ridden him, and he had been in several clinics. We had done quite a lot together, but the trailer-loading was still stressful for both of us.

Because I can sense and feel so much, I often think the stress that was created for me was feeling the stress from him, but in retrospect, I realized I had my own trauma. About two years after Corazon got his leg pinched by the trailer door, I had an accident where I rolled my pickup truck. I'll never forget being in that aluminum metal box watching the curve come up on the road, feeling my tires lose traction, and knowing in a split second what was ahead of me. As I was stuck in that metal box, I remember all time slowing down and I watched out the window as the truck rolled, and at one point, I was upside-down with snow out my window, and then suddenly, upright again. The crunching and heaving of the metal was something that stayed with me. Luckily, I walked away from that accident. But, as you might have suspected, the effects were long-lasting. To this day I am still not a very good passenger, especially on winding mountain roads.

So here I was with my wild horse who had been captured and put into a metal box and taken away from his life as he knew it. And I had my trauma of experiencing being trapped in a metal box with no way out, even when the pickup stopped upright and I knew I could get out. Everything within that truck had been banging and flying around as well. Both Corazon and I had our trauma around metal boxes. At that point, I decided it might be a good time to take a break from the engagement with the metal box. I started my healing process and Corazon got a lot of time off. He was not asked to go into the metal box for approximately three years. Then, things changed at the ranch and I ended up getting a beautiful champagne palomino horse named Layla. I picked her up from an individual who had lost his home in the floods that hit the Front Range area of Colorado in September of 2013. She was pregnant when I got her, and she gave birth to her foal here at the ranch. I named the little filly Ginger.

Ginger was a hoot, and it astounded me to find out what it was like to train a filly from birth. The only reference I had in training a horse was working with this wild mustang stallion that had been gelded when he came in from the wild at five and a half years old. A friend referred me to a very kind trainer by the name of Tim who was known for his work with foals. I needed his help with Ginger because, of course, I realized I had no idea what to do with this little thing. As adorable as she was, I was a bit lost. Tim and I had great fun working with this little horse. Little Ginger helped me get beyond a lot of my fears of horses. Tim would teach me different methods of communication. We would watch her digest and understand what we were asking. She was very gregarious, willing, outward, and daring. She was quite a joy to work with and would catch on to things very quickly. Hardly ever would she pull back, rear up, or stand and refuse, actions that I had become so accustomed to experiencing with Corazon.

When it was time to teach Ginger how to trailer-load, it went very smoothly. The very first time we showed the trailer to her, Ginger stepped up and went in. Of course, I couldn't believe my eyes. The more I worked with her, the more I realized just how profoundly difficult it had been to work with Corazon. As we were working with Ginger to get her to load well, I also started to work with her mom, Layla. I knew, eventually, that Layla would have to go to a new home, and I wanted her to be an agreeable horse to a new owner. I had seen her be trailer-loaded only once when she almost knocked down the man loading her to bring her to my place. Again, in a little metal box.

I decided, intentionally, that I would put Corazon in a paddock, and then I'd park the trailer right next to the paddock. I'd play with Ginger and have her get up into the trailer and give her all sorts of treats and say nice things to her and pet her and groom her outside of the box. She'd get all of my attention, and I'd always make it very happy and appreciative and loving. I also had a pedestal that I knew Corazon loved to get up on, so I had it off to the side and Ginger would put her front feet on the pedestal and I'd stroke her back. She'd look proud, like a big girl. Corazon would stand right at the fence, not moving an inch. He would stare, intently watching every single move.

After Ginger and I had these great sessions, I'd give her a nice bowl of goodies and then off to the paddock she'd go. I could sense by the way Corazon was looking at me that there was jealousy building. Even though he'd been a complicated horse and we'd had many tiring conversations, he still considered me to be part of his herd; in a way, one of his mares. I could tell he was jealous of the attention I was giving another herd member.

I'd do the same with Layla that I'd done with Ginger. Layla didn't take long to get used to the trailer, and I'd give her kudos; it was all a lovely experience. When she got into the trailer, I'd have a bag of feed waiting and give her a more positive experience. Some trainers would say to never give treats or hang a bag to entice a horse. If they are going into the trailer, they should go because you asked them. In my mind, I want to make things easy for my horses so they get used to things. It doesn't mean they'll get that bag of hay every time they go in but, by all means, if they can have a positive experience of enjoying food while they're in the trailer, I'm going to give that to them.

There are many ways to train a horse, which can be one of the most confusing parts of being a new horse owner. It can be very confusing because you'll do what you learned from one trainer and the next trainer will tell you you're doing it wrong, or there is a better way. If you have perfectionist tendencies it is very frustrating. You may feel like you're never getting anything right, bringing down your self-esteem.

I watched Corazon and I saw the envy and jealousy. I saw him watching and realized it would be a bit sneaky for me to capitalize on his jealousy, but I decided to anyway. After I worked with Ginger and Layla for several days and he started to paw with his front hoof on the fence as if saying, "What about me?" I brought him out. Lo and behold, the very first time I asked him, he went into the metal box. He stood perfectly and ate some hay.

For several days after, I kept practicing trailer-loading with him, and he had all sorts of good experiences. Some days were more difficult than others. Sometimes I'd only have thirty minutes and he could sense that pressure of time. Any sort of pressure around that trailer, and he would not want to go in. Eventually, he was jumping in and out and there was no big deal.

About a year later, I decided to take him to a very big clinic. Frederick Pignon from France was coming in with his wife, Magali Delgado. I was taking Corazon to work with Frederick and learn more liberty work. Corazon and I had become rather dull together. We were doing EFLC programs, and I could tell Corazon was pretty darn bored, and to be honest, so was I. Many of the things I'd wanted to achieve with him had been pushed aside to build my business and to serve all these other human beings. Both my herd and I were quite weary.

I had to think of a new tactic for loading because I knew I'd have some stress and anxiety getting him into the trailer and to the clinic by myself. My new tactic was one many trainers would also nay-say and criticize. But again, I thought to myself, *The trailer is something that Corazon views as traumatic.* Getting into the trailer with the metal sounds of clanging can put him into a trauma response, which is to whip back around and jump out.

Slowly, through these processes, I was helping him de-traumatize, to develop a new behavior under the stimulation of the original trauma. However, the original trauma was so deep, it took a while to alleviate the initial responses. Getting to the root of the trauma might be a lifetime of work, just as it has been for me. There are still certain things that trigger me back into the fear response.

I felt lucky that I could understand the impact of being in a metal box at a similar level as Corazon. So, the tactic for this particular incident was to open up part of the paddock, back up the trailer, and let that trailer sit there for him to go in and out at will and as he desired. Every evening, I'd put a bowl of his grain and a pile of hay out for him. The first night, I put just the grain inside with hay outside. Eventually, I put all hay and grain inside. If he wanted to eat, he had to get in the trailer. But all night long he had the choice to look around, go in and come out, listen to his hooves on the floor, bang around and not hurt himself as he got the lay of the land. Eventually, he'd just get in and out of the trailer with no problem. Some mornings I would come out and he would be waiting inside the trailer for his food. It was quite fascinating to watch.

As you can imagine, the day of the clinic, I just walked him into the trailer. He stood peacefully inside. I got out, shut the door, and off to the clinic we went. Now, I'd love to tell you I never had any problems trailering him again. However, after four days of being at the clinic, I was nervous that I would not be able to get him into the trailer to get home. I felt the pressure. I decided to have a cup of coffee so I would be alert and ready to drive in the dark. Once again, this horse's high sensing abilities picked up on this contracted energy in my body, and when I went to load him for home, he refused to get into the trailer. At this point, I tried three or four times, and then I got it. My body was filled with adrenaline from the coffee and I was tense because I wanted to get it done. But I wasn't going to stand there and try to get him to do something that I knew he was probably going to fight, not because he didn't know how to get in the trailer but because of the quality of energy I was presenting while asking him to load into the trailer.

So, I went back and found a young lady who'd never loaded him before, but I'd watched her with her horses, and she was lovely and kind and sweet and dear. I asked if she'd help me, and off to the trailer we went. She had no problem energetically. She talked to him a moment, circled a little bit, and then asked him to get into the trailer, and in he went. He and I headed home. I had a mixture of frustration followed by relief to be heading out, and then amusement due to the complicated nature of this little wild Spanish mustang.

There are many ways to understand the influences of working with these magnificent beings, in particular wild mustangs. Mentally, Corazon is a very intelligent horse. On an energetic level, he is highly tuned, so if his handler is tense, anxious, or uncertain, he is going to respond to that energy. He will have more questions and not be quite as willing to do what is being asked of him. There are also the past events that influence us, whether we are human or horse. How do we work through the traumas of our history to move into what the future is demanding? Who do we trust and why?

Corazon has taught me that when you are a wild horse such as a highly sensing and intelligent horse like him, who you trust and why can change on a dime. When it's play and joy and fun, I have him in my back pocket. But any level of tension in my body amplifies for him and he will have a lot of questions. This is part of our dance in relationship. He's not the perfect horse and I'm not the perfect human. As many trainers told me when I first got Corazon, I had no right to have him. And they might have been right, but they could also be absolutely wrong.

Corazon and I have found our work in the world. He and I have found how to navigate daily challenges together. He has taught me what it means to be a family with a wild one. He has taught me what it means to be un-domesticated. He has shown me my edges of fear and anxiety and how it affects our relationship. He has taught me what it means to be strong, to have my inner freedom, to sense another and their intentions, and to know what it's like to move through dramatic transitions and painful past events. Both he and I have had to learn that if we allow the past to run us then, indeed, we live trapped in metal boxes. We must, step by step, figure out how to heal the past and live in the world of today, even if it is not the world that we chose. He evokes in me an understanding that the freedom I seek from the metal boxes of my body and mind may be found in the wildness of the mountains where the vast land and nature can penetrate every cell of my body. But the reality is, the true freedom from the metal boxes of the past can only be found deep within me as I learn to control and align my entire being.

I still have one fantasy about Corazon de la Montana. I wish I could stand at the edge of a vast green meadow filled with a herd of multicolored wild horses and a snowcapped mountain range beyond. I would be just like Frank Hopkins portrayed in the movie *Hidalgo*. I would say my thank you to Corazon, remove his halter, and set him free—just as he has done for me.

REFLECTIONS

Every relationship is a dance; a dance of understanding the other, who you are in relationship to the other, and seeing how the other magnifies something within you. Horses are amazing, giving beings and they are also mirrors of another being's consciousness. Corazon and I mirror each other's old traumas, fears, and concerns. When we get rabbled up, knotted up, and the dance is of confusion, I've learned that sometimes that it's best to step away and come back when the dance can be filled with more lightness and joy. Does this put limitations on what we can do? Absolutely. But what I thought we were meant to do might not be what we are here to do.

- How does your horse mirror you?
- What have you wondered about your horse's behavior that gives you a glimpse of how you are in the world?
- What kind of relationship dance are you in with your horse?
- What trauma have you had that might be reflected in your horse?
- How do you see working through that trauma with your horse?
- What new perspectives have you learned about yourself from your horse?
- What can you learn by imagining your horse's past?

Choices

The late July day was beautiful and sunny, with white puffy clouds floating in a light blue sky. The hawks were flying freely in the air, and the squirrels were running about in liveliness. All of the hay recently cut in the fields lay drying or in bales waiting to be picked up. The freshness of the early summer was declining as the late summer harvest approached.

The day was hot, with a touch of mugginess, slowing us all down as we hung out at the ranch for a program with the horses. The group sat in a circle and introduced themselves before I began the lectures. It is always interesting to learn where people come from, what interests them the most with the horses, and what they intend to experience during the day. The group is always diverse in age, background, and desires, and this one was no different. Seldom do we have men in the group, and I still feel so fortunate when I do. Having a man in the group is a lovely balance of energy because they bring in a different perspective, thought process, and way of being in the world.

Ben, a participant, was a seventy-five-year-old man who had done an extensive amount of personal work. He had a library of books on personal growth and quantum mechanics. I could tell that Ben wanted to add more knowledge to every lecture I offered the group. He sat politely and digested what I said, and I could sense his eagerness to contribute. He was clearly a person who wanted to give.

This group was rather quiet, but they came together and connected quickly. I could hardly wait to bring them to the horses to see how my horses would interact with them and what sort of lessons were going to be offered to these humans throughout the day. It's always fascinating to watch because no two people and horse pairs are the same. The sensitive and responsive nature of horses helps people understand their behavioral patterns and often their deepest desires.

I prepared the group for time with the horses by letting them know and learn about the way of the horse. I taught them about the herd dynamics and what motivates horses within the herd and with each other, and I invited them to step into being more horse-like, as they were going to experience the horses in their round pen sessions. The horses were at the peak of their health in the middle of the summer. Summer is a slow time where they get to stroll in the pastures, eat green grass to their heart's desire, mingle with each other, and be in the rhythm of life. Seldom do they struggle, as the weather is consistent, and their bones become lazy in the heat of the day. They are content and harmonious, and also very willing to begin their work with the people who have come to learn from them.

Ben was very enthusiastic about the wild horses and horses in general. Although he was seventy-five, Ben's enthusiasm for his experience was palpable. I envied that he was living his life to the fullest and embracing his intuition to arrive at the workshop and do work he'd never done before and experience the horses in a new way.

The horse Ben picked to work with was Corazon de la Montana, a mustang who was wild until he was five and a half years old. Corazon carries a tremendous amount of strength and power within his presence. He knows precisely what he stands for; there is no doubt in his mind of who he is. He has clarity about what he wants and how he wishes to express himself. I have never seen doubt in this horse's eye. That is not Corazon's demeanor. He has confidence in a way I've never experienced.

The session began in the afternoon. The day was changing slightly as more clouds were coming in. Luckily for us, we had the shade of the cottonwood trees around the round pen area where we'd work. Additionally, a slight breeze had begun. Everybody was so happy to be out with the horses for the entire afternoon. We had already gone through many activities with the horses, but that afternoon would be filled with the individual sessions, and people loved those sessions.

Ben and Corazon did their work together late in the afternoon. I stood near the round pen, with Corazon already inside. Corazon stood at the edge of the rail, just in front of all of the participants. The participants were sitting in plastic lawn chairs only four feet outside the round pen. Each had a journal to take notes of what they discovered even in watching another person with the horse. I often say that those outside the round pen can have an equally if not more powerful experience than the person who goes into the round pen with the horse. This particular round pen proved that concept.

Ben stepped up with me, and we walked to the gate. As we did so, Corazon sauntered away and began to walk around the round pen as close to the fence as possible, creating distance between him and Ben and myself. As Ben and I stood outside the round pen, I invited him to become more aware of his body, feelings, and thinking patterns. I invited him to become more horse-like. Ben willingly allowed me to guide him through this process with many questions as he continued to focus on himself.

I watched Corazon as he continued to stay at the far end of the round pen, glancing off into the field to the horses that were several pastures away. He was still not interested in engaging with us; the other horses far away held his attention. As I glanced at Ben, I noticed that his hands, hanging at his side, trembled. I sensed Ben was feeling fear, vulnerability, or anxiety. I continued to work with Ben, and eventually, he revealed that he was feeling a lot of different energy in his body. We talked about this so he could have the clarity to focus and have the level of confidence that Corazon demonstrated daily.

Ben was more than willing to continue to listen to his body and be on the journey of exploration with me. Eventually, he was able to identify that he was feeling a mixture of trepidation and excitement. The allure of Corazon and his stallion-like tendencies and energy magnified for Ben. There was something about this wild horse that ignited something within Ben that had laid dormant for a long time.

Ben finally came to his heart as we gazed at Corazon, and he continued to talk about all the feelings and thoughts running through his body and head. As he focused on his heart, and he took a few breaths, his eyes softly landed on Corazon, and I sensed a shift in Ben. At that precise moment, Corazon turned away from the rail and walked toward Ben, no longer interested in the horses frolicking in the field. Corazon now wanted to connect with Ben.

Ben took a couple of deep breaths as he took in the splendor and beauty of the black horse walking gently toward him. As he centered attention on his heart space, I began to ask him questions about his life and what he desired most from his heart. Corazon walked across the round pen until finally, he stopped right in front of us. Ben and I were still outside the rail. As Corazon stared at us, Ben shared that he had recently remarried, and he loved this woman very much and would do anything for her. She had children from her first marriage who lived locally and she wanted to spend as much time with them and her grandchildren as possible. She was requesting that Ben accompany her to all of the grandchildren's baseball, soccer, and other outings.

Although Ben loved children and his wife very much, he was struggling with this desire she was expressing and the demands she was putting on him. Ben wanted to make her happy, and he loved his new grandchildren, but it was all too much for him. What Ben wanted was to finally step into something he felt passionate about. Ben, now retired, was ready to live his life more fully. Ben didn't have that many years left to be agile, out moving freely in nature. He was feeling internal pressure to live his life fully while honoring his spouse's values and being able to have shared time together.

I helped him process the confusing emotions about this relationship and what was bubbling up in it. Corazon continued to stand there, softly unmoving, unflinching, his eyes resting on Ben. Ben also stood very still with his eyes resting on Corazon. I began to ask Ben about his deepest desires. Because Corazon was now engaged and ready to connect with Ben, I invited Ben to step into the pen.

Ben stood still in front of Corazon, and I invited Ben to connect with Corazon on a physical level. He had yet to touch this beautiful horse that had walked up to him. I noticed a slight tremble in his hand, and I didn't worry about it, because I knew from Corazon's body language that it didn't matter how Ben was feeling, Corazon was there to support him. As Ben began to stroke Corazon's shiny black back, I continued to talk with Ben. I asked him, if he could live the life he wanted to live, what would he do differently? He replied that he'd spend more time with horses. I asked him to tell me more. He began to talk about his love for horses ever since he was a small boy, how their incredible beauty moved him deeply. Ben spoke compassionately about wild horses that once lived freely on public lands that are captured and forced into captivity, such as Corazon. He expressed how he wanted to embody that same sense of unabashed freedom to move physically on the land and feel the stability and power that the wild horses represented. As he talked, I noticed his eyes were beginning to tear up. Corazon lowered his head ever so slightly and began to lick and chew. The moment of realization was potent.

At a deeper level, I think Ben realized he was at a turning point in his life, a point where he may not have the opportunity to run free on the earth like a wild stallion, like Corazon, who once ran wild and free in the mountains of Montana. Ben continued to speak about his love of the mustangs, and as he did, Corazon turned his body and came up along the side of Ben. They stood next to each other, and then suddenly, Corazon very smoothly began to lower his body. He folded his front legs underneath himself, so his knees were right at Ben's feet, and then he lowered the rest of his body onto the warm sand. Like a cat or a dog at his master's feet, Corazon gently laid himself down as Ben stood quietly with tears rolling down his face.

Ben, who had not had a lot of horse experience, did not recognize the significance of what this wild horse did in his presence. When Corazon and I first met, he would never have laid down in the presence of a human being, no matter how far away he was from the human. As we talked about Corazon and his journey, Ben began to understand the significance of what Corazon's gesture demonstrated. On some level, Corazon was validating Ben's deep desire to connect with horses and to live a passion he'd never embraced. Corazon was the horse at the master's feet, a difficult thing for Ben to embrace.

On an emotional level, I could see the waves of recognition moving through Ben. I could see his heart shifting and opening. I could see him lost in the process of awakening. Through our conversation, Ben began to acknowledge the importance of his passion unlived and the gentle gesture of this little wild horse. Tears streamed down as he spoke about what he would do. Ben wanted to be with the horses every day. He wanted to be around them and part of the herd. Because he was also a mentor for men, he had the desire to experience what it would be like to support others in being with these beautiful, magnificent, powerful creatures as teachers in their leadership.

The realization of the authentic dream of his most profound passion and what was unlived was almost more than Ben could hold. Corazon continued to lay at his feet, his chin now resting in the warm sand. His breath was long and deep, and he was going into a more integrated sleep experience. In all of my years facilitating the EFLC sessions with my herd, and in particular this once wild horse, I had never seen Corazon offer this gesture. I had never seen him so relaxed and with such grace and ease as he lay at a person's feet.

It was odd to me that Ben was standing only about three feet from the edge of the rail, so when Corazon lay down, he was unable to lay back on his side. Instead, he remained at Ben's feet with his front legs curled under him and his chin resting on the sand. We stood there for quite some time. We would talk a bit, and then there were long segments of pure silence. I invited Ben to listen to Corazon's breath and feel his feet on the hot sand, to find a place that he could rest with what was in the moment. I invited Ben to breathe with Corazon and to allow this awakening and realization of his truth to be alive within his being.

Ben was glad to have those opportunities. His heart was fully open. Even as a facilitator with fifteen years of experience, I could feel tears welling up in my eyes. The gentle masculine energy in front of me in Ben and demonstrated by my once wild stallion mustang was potent. When I glanced at the others sitting outside the round pen, sensing how palpable the emotion was, how quiet the group was, I noticed several dabbing their eyes with tissues. Behind them, the rest of my herd stood in a row along the fence line, each watching with soft, gazing eyes. It was as if we moved into a space that transcended all time. It was as if each of us had our hearts opened to another level that we had not experienced before.

I knew that this session for Ben was about him having a palpable experience of grounded heart energy with the kindred spirit of a wild horse, something that his whole being had been crying for his entire life, and that finally, at the age of seventy-five, he was experiencing. I wish I could tell you that I received a letter from Ben months later. I wish I could tell you how he had entered into an equine program and was now leading young men with horses, teaching them leadership and emotional intelligence skills. I wish I could tell you that he bought a ranch and was living the dream he had never lived his entire life because he had always done what was right for the family.

Unfortunately, it seems that it did not happen for Ben. Although he recognized that his true self wanted the horses, their essence, and the experience of them to be in his life on a day-to-day basis, Ben once again chose something else. I did hear from him months later. He sent me beautiful books for Christmas, and I was touched. But there was a part of me that was sad that my horse did not open Ben's heart enough, or show him enough. Or that Ben did not fully understand the potent gesture of my wild mustang, and that that gesture did not support Ben in making a different life choice. Ben focused his life on serving his new wife, traveling with her, and going to many baseball and soccer games. A noble choice based in love.

Who am I to say that it should be any different for Ben? In those moments with Corazon lying at his feet, Ben touched on the part of himself that needed to come to the surface and be recognized. A dream came to fruition, if only for those forty minutes. All of us have particular dreams and desires in our life, and many times we suppress those to fill the roles we feel we need to fulfill for our families, for our jobs, for whoever in our life we feel a responsibility. And on the journey to filling those roles, we often lose the essence of who we are. We lose our passions, our desires, our way.

When it's all said and done, we can't name what is wrong or right. All we can know is that we lived our life in the way we thought was appropriate. We made concessions where we chose to make them, and we adapted where circumstances required us to change. In the end, what will always be true is that our most authentic essence, the being we are truly meant to be, the truth of our nature, is still within us. Just as Corazon has never changed in his core, he has never changed who he is at that spiritual, emotional level, it is the same for all of us. Whether Corazon is wild and free on the land or in the round pen, his essence never wavers.

I know that that day in the round pen with Corazon, Ben received an awakening, an opening, and an exchange of benevolent, masculine energy from a passionate, once wild horse. What I know to be true is that this experience will never be taken away from Ben. He will always go back to that memory of how a little black horse laying at his feet, resting, brought him back to his heart.

REFLECTIONS

We all strive for more freedom in our lives. Often, our highest desires are not achieved through external circumstances. In a gentle and profound way, Corazon offered a kinship to Ben. Corazon demonstrated that he resonated deeply with Ben and offered a gesture of complete relaxation and recognition to Ben. By giving him this experience, Ben was able to have a deep heart-opening experience.

- Where in your life can you find that support for yourself?
- Have you had an experience with a horse or other being that reflected exactly what you needed to make a new choice?
- Have you learned to say no when doing so might affect others?
- When is it time to move forward? When is it time to rest?
- What would change in your life if you began to make different choices for yourself?

Acknowledgments

I would like to thank Nicole Mele at Skyhorse Publishing for extending the invitation to write this book. Nicole was a joy to work with and the process was very smooth. Additional appreciation goes out to the team at Skyhorse Publishing for their contributions in making the book come to fruition. I would not have accepted the invitation without a conversation with Natalie Collins. Her perspective guided me to commit to writing this book, even while I was still completing another book. MJ Schwader patiently supported me through the writing journey. His expertise in editing, transcribing my stories, and aiding in the shaping of the reflections portion was invaluable.

Francis Rico, in a way no other human being has, always reflects the essence of my being and the depth of my connection with nature's beautiful horses. His validation lifts me and magically fills me with ease and joy. Shelley Royendyk's wise support has been and always will be invaluable. Barbara Novak, soul sister, has always supported my writing and path as a healer for both humans and horses. John Baker's belief in me during the early days with Corazon kept me grounded during rocky times. Ariana Strozzi Mazzucchi, I am appreciative that this book has reconnected us and our shared vision.

I would also like to thank the thousands of individuals who have experienced horses as teachers and healers through my programs. Your trust in me and the horses we worked with is deeply gratifying. The following individuals helped significantly to shape the stories in this book, my appreciation for your openness and vulnerability is unwavering. Thank you to: Judy Wellfare, Casey Jordon, Crystal Zinn, Carlos Eduardo Mesa, Pedro Miguel Estrada Londoño, Bruce Iverson, Annik Goudsmet, Anna Harold, and Nadine Delire. Aldo Civico, words cannot convey the respect I have for you and the joy I have experienced in our co-creations with horses.

Many people have helped me with my horses and have come to my aid when I needed them. You helped to shape the stories I have shared. You know who you are, and my horses and I thank you for your time, energy, caring, and services. A special thank you goes to Hugh Coleby, Tim Van Donselaar, Jaime Jeremy Wade, Ginger Kathrens, Frederic Pignon, and Susan Gibbs (as you rest in peace).

The individuals who have worked for many years behind the scenes have supported me in being an advocate for equine intelligence through my books, videos, and programs. Tracy Shiflett and Lynette Dominquez have made massive contributions in supporting me in bringing this work into the world. Maddie Shirk, thank you for the excellent care you give my herd, dog, and home, and the joyful giggles we share about their antics.

Deep appreciation goes out to all of the individuals who studied the way of the horse in my yearlong EFLC certification program. A very special gratefulness goes to those graduates who returned to support new students coming into the program. Your dedication to horses and to others has not gone unseen.

I want to say to all of the horses who I have been blessed to know, regardless if it was for an hour, a weekend, or many years, each of you speaks to me in a way no other human or creature has. Forgive me for the times I have not heard you or understand you correctly, as it was not my intention. May this book elevate all humans who may interact with you and help them see and experience you and all horses in a different light. May all who read this book glean the profound spiritual connection possible that I have attempted to convey in this book and through your teachings, the way of the horse.

About Kathy Pike

Founder of The Academy for Coaching with Horses, Kathy Pike is a speaker, coach, facilitator, and author of *Hope . . . From the Heart of Horses: How Horses Teach Us About Presence, Strength, and Awareness*. Kathy created the vision and was a founding partner of the *Horse as Teacher* series, featuring two books that each highlighted ten authors. Her first book, *Pathways to a Radiant Self: A Journey of Growth and Discovery with the Chakras*, offers a complete guide for healing and expanding one's energy field. Kathy has over twenty-seven years of experience in the areas of personal development, intuitive reading, healing, life coaching, equine-based learning, and leadership development.

Kathy brought her extensive experience in healing knowledge and her love of horses to the world of equine facilitated learning to become a pioneer in Equine Facilitated Learning and Coaching (EFLC). She has taught EFLC Certification Programs around the world, having trained others to employ Horse as a guide and mentor for the human heart and spirit in more than eighteen countries.

Kathy's compassionate, intuitive, and cutting-edge approach draws out her clients' deepest levels of truth, power, and ability to live with purpose and passion. Her diverse approach to accessing human potential has grown from her experience as a coach trainer for CoachU, a corporate trainer, a teacher at the Boulder College of Massage Therapy, and ten years working in the healing arts as a massage and polarity therapist.

Kathy has spent extensive time in the wilderness, developing a deep respect for Mother Earth, the four elements, and all creatures. Her experiences in the areas of life coaching, outdoor adventure, and healing modalities create a perfect foundation for her journey and work with horses.

Kathy's most recent book *Horse Spirits Speak: On Love, Presence, and Harmony in a Chaotic World* is a collection of channeled messages from horse spirits. With her experiences in nature, her knowledge of healing, and her deep connection with horses, Kathy is a perfect vessel for the horse spirits to bring their messages to the world.